Love Poems

Publisher and Creative Director: Nick Wells
Project Editor and Selection: Chelsea Edwards
Designer: Mike Spender

FLAME TREE PUBLISHING
Crabtree Hall, Crabtree Lane
Fulham, London SW6 6TY
United Kingdom

www.flametreepublishing.com

First published in 2007

11 13 14 12

3 5 7 9 10 8 6 4 2

Flame Tree is part of The Foundry Creative Media Company Limited

A CIP record for this book is available from the British Library.

ISBN: 978-184451-708-4

Every effort has been made to contact copyright holders. We apologize
in advance for any omissions and would be pleased to insert the
appropriate acknowledgement in subsequent editions of this publication.

While every endeavour has been made to ensure the accuracy of the
reproduction of the images in this book, we would be grateful to receive
any comments or suggestions for inclusion in future reprints.

Printed in Singapore

Thanks to: Kelly Fenlon, Chris Herbert and Claire Walker

Love

Poems

A special selection edited by
C.N. Edwards

FLAME TREE
PUBLISHING

Contents

Introduction

Love has been the focus of poems since the inception of poetry itself, and shows no signs of dissipating. Love is an intensely charged emotion that forces expression in its most raw and potent form. From the height of elation to the depths of heartbreak, love inspires polar opposites as well as all the shades in between.

This anthology ranges from the eloquence of sixteenth-century writers Christopher Marlowe (1564–93) and William Shakespeare (1564–1616) to the works of Romanticism's pioneers, Percy Bysshe Shelley (1792–1822) and Lord Byron (1788–1824). Love has been charted by these staple literary figures as well as countless others and yet retains its elusive nature. Love evades definition; each new devotee experiences it in an entirely new capacity.

Love's guises are so convincing that the identification of love itself has become a substantial component of romantic poetry. It is a task that has been undertaken by both Katherine Mansfield (1888–1923) and Armenian poet Bedros Tourian (1851–72). Mansfield's poem 'Secret Flowers' concerns itself with the varying intensity of love, and what that shift implies for her relationship to love.

Also included in this collection are the poetic works of famed artists Michelangelo Buonarroti (1475–1564) and Dante Gabriel Rossetti (1828–82). Moreover the latter is represented not only by his poetry, but also by his exquisite paintings that contributed greatly to the Pre-Raphaelite art movement. Rossetti's sister, Christina Georgina Rossetti (1830–94), also makes a substantial contribution to this collection with her poignant work. Her poem 'Remember' is haunting in its beauty as the protagonist selflessly encourages her lover not to grieve for her once she has passed away.

As a poetic subject, love is an enduring one that refuses to be confined to any single style or genre of writing. Instead it has featured in the work of Transcendentalist Ralph Waldo Emerson (1803–82), Modernist Rainer Maria Rilke (1875–1926) and famed Gothic writer Edgar Allan Poe (1809–49). Poets' expression of love is chameleonic and consequently caters to a vast audience.

Shakespeare is featured heavily throughout as he addresses the pinnacles and pitfalls that love creates. Extracts from his plays enable the reader to celebrate the blossoming of a nascent love as well as observe those that 'lov'd not wisely, but too well'. Shakespeare's sonnets and plays are frequently based around the trials and tribulations of love, further propounding the human need and desire to experience love.

Contained within this collection are some of the most popular love poems ever written, including Andrew Marvell's (1621–78) 'To His Coy Mistress' and Robert Burns' (1759–96) 'A Red, Red Rose'. Split into six chapters this anthology features a vast array of romantic poetry. Beginning with new love and celebration, the collection continues to evolve through love's tragedies ending in the reminiscence of lost love. From across the world and the centuries, this anthology delivers poetry spanning the gamut of love's emotions in an attempt to encapsulate love's beautiful and treacherous journey, wherever you may be on it.

NASCENT LOVE

The Passionate Shepherd to His Love

Come live with me and be my love,
And we will all the pleasures prove,
That valleys, groves, hills and fields,
Woods or steepy mountains yields.

And we will sit upon the rocks,
Seeing the shepherds feed their flocks
By shallow rivers, to whose falls
Melodious birds sing madrigals.

And I will make thee beds of roses,
And a thousand fragrant posies,
A cap of flowers and a kirtle
Embroidered all with leaves of myrtle;

A gown made of the finest wool,
Which from our pretty lambs we pull;
Fair-lined slippers for the cold,
With buckles of the purest gold;

A belt of straw and ivy buds,
With coral clasps and amber studs;
And if these pleasures may thee move,
Come live with me and be my love.

NASCENT LOVE

The shepherd swains shall dance and sing
For thy delight each May morning;
If these delights thy mind may move,
Then live with me and be my love.

Christopher Marlowe (1564–93)

Who Ever Loved, That Loved Not at First Sight

It lies not in our power to love or hate,
For will in us is overruled by fate.
When two are stripped, long ere the course begin,
We wish that one should love, the other win;
And one especially do we affect
Of two gold ingots, like in each respect:
The reason no man knows; let it suffice
What we behold is censured by our eyes.
Where both deliberate, the love is slight:
Who ever loved, that loved not at first sight?

Christopher Marlowe (1564–93)

O Mistress Mine

O Mistress mine, where are you roaming?
O stay and hear! your true-love's coming
That can sing both high and low;
Trip no further, pretty sweeting,
Journeys end in lovers' meeting–
Every wise man's son doth know.

What is love? 'tis not hereafter;
Present mirth hath present laughter;
What's to come is still unsure:
In delay there lies no plenty,–
Then come kiss me, Sweet-and-twenty,
Youth's a stuff will not endure.

William Shakespeare (1564–1616)

Extract from Romeo and Juliet Act 2 Scene II

What light through yonder window breaks?
It is east, and Juliet is the sun.
Arise, fair sun, and kill the envious moon,
Who is already sick and pale with grief
That thou her maid art far more fair than she.
Be not her maid, since she is envious;
Her vestal livery is but sick and green,
And none but fools do wear it; cast it off.
It is my lady; O, it is my love!
O that she knew she were!
She speaks, yet she says nothing. What of that?
Her eye discourses; I will answer it.
I am too bold 'tis not to me she speaks;
Two of the fairest stars in all heaven,
Having some business, do entreat her eyes
To twinkle in their spheres till they return.
What if her eyes were there, they in her head?
The brightness of her cheek would shame those stars,
As daylight doth a lamp; her eyes in heaven
Would through the airy region stream so bright
That birds would sing, and think it were not night
See how she leans her cheek upon her hand!
O that I were a glove upon that hand,
That I might touch that cheek!

William Shakespeare (1564–1616)

To Celia

Drinke to me, onely, with thine eyes.
  And I will pledge with mine;
Or leave a kisse but in the cup,
  And I'll not look for wine.
The thirst that from the soule doth rise,
  Doth aske a drink divine:
But might I of Jove's Nectar sup,
  I would not change for thine.
I sent thee, late, a rosie wreath,
  Not so much honouring thee,
As giving it a hope, that there
  It could not withered bee.
But thou thereon did'st onely breath,
  And sen'st it backe to me:
Since when it growes, and smells, I sweare,
  Not of it selfe, but thee.

Benjamin Jonson (1572–1637)

There is a Lady Sweet and Kind

There is a lady sweet and kind,
Was never face so pleas'd my mind;
I did but see her passing by,
And yet I love her till I die.

Her gesture, motion, and her smiles,
Her wit, her voice, my heart beguiles,
Beguiles my heart, I know not why,
And yet I love her till I die.

Her free behaviour, winning looks,
Will make a lawyer burn his books;
I touch'd her not, alas! not I,
And yet I love her till I die.
Had I her fast betwixt mine arms,
Judge you that think such sports were harms,
Were't any harm? no, no, fie, fie,
For I will love her till I die.

Should I remain confined there
So long as Phoebus in his sphere,
I to request, she to deny,
Yet would I love her till I die.

Cupid is winged and doth range,
Her country so my love doth change:
But change she earth, or change she sky,
Yet will I love her till I die.

Thomas Ford (1580–1648)

Wooing Song

Love is the blossom where there blows
Every thing that lives or grows:
Love doth make the Heav'ns to move,
And the Sun doth burn in love:
Love the strong and weak doth yoke,
And makes the ivy climb the oak,
Under whose shadows lions wild,
Soften'd by love, grow tame and mild:
Love no med'cine can appease,
He burns the fishes in the seas:
Not all the skill his wounds can stench,
Not all the sea his fire can quench.
Love did make the bloody spear
Once a leavy coat to wear,
While in his leaves there shrouded lay
Sweet birds, for love that sing and play
And of all love's joyful flame
I the bud and blossom am.
Only bend thy knee to me,
Thy wooing shall thy winning be!

See, see the flowers that below
Now as fresh as morning blow;
And of all the virgin rose
That as bright Aurora shows;
How they all unleavèd die,
Losing their virginity!
Like unto a summer shade,
But now born, and now they fade.

Every thing doth pass away;
There is danger in delay:
Come, come, gather then the rose,
Gather it, or it you lose!
All the sand of Tagus' shore
Into my bosom casts his ore:
All the valleys' swimming corn
To my house is yearly borne:
Every grape of every vine
Is gladly bruised to make me wine:
While ten thousand kings, as proud,
To carry up my train have bow'd,
And a world of ladies send me
In my chambers to attend me:
All the stars in Heav'n that shine,
And ten thousand more, are mine:
Only bend thy knee to me,
Thy wooing shall thy winning be!

Giles Fletcher (1586–1623)

To Electra

I dare not ask a kiss,
I dare not beg a smile,
Lest having that, or this,
I might grow proud the while.

No, no, the utmost share
Of my desire shall be
Only to kiss that air
That lately kissèd thee.

Robert Herrick (1591–1674)

To His Coy Mistress

Had we but World enough, and Time,
This coyness Lady were no crime.
We would sit down, and think which way
To walk, and pass our long Loves Day.
Thou by the Indian Ganges side
Should'st Rubies find: I by the Tide
Of Humber would complain. I would
Love you ten years before the Flood:
And you should if you please refuse
Till the Conversion of the Jews.
My vegetable Love should grow
Vaster then Empires, and more slow.
An hundred years should go to praise
Thine Eyes, and on thy Forehead Gaze.
Two hundred to adore each Breast:
But thirty thousand to the rest.
An Age at least to every part,
And the last Age should show your Heart.
For Lady you deserve this State;
Nor would I love at lower rate.
But at my back I alwaies hear
Times winged Charriot hurrying near:
And yonder all before us lye
DesErts of vast Eternity.
Thy Beauty shall no more be found;
Nor, in thy marble Vault, shall sound
My ecchoing Song: then Worms shall try
That long preserv'd Virginity:
And your quaint Honour turn to dust;

And into ashes all my Lust.
The Grave's a fine and private place,
But none I think do there embrace.
Now therefore, while the youthful hew
Sits on thy skin like morning dew
And while thy willing Soul transpires
At every pore with instant Fires,
Now let us sport us while we may;
And now, like am'rous birds of prey,
Rather at once our Time devour,
Than languish in his slow-chapt pow'r.
Let us roll all our Strength, and all
Our sweetness, up into one Ball:
And tear our Pleasures with rough strife,
Through the Iron gates of Life.
Thus, though we cannot make our Sun
Stand still, yet we will make him run.

Andrew Marvell (1621–78)

Ah, How Sweet it is to Love

Ah, how sweet it is to love!
Ah, how gay is young Desire!
And what pleasing pains we prove
When we first approach Love's fire!
Pains of love be sweeter far
Than all other pleasures are.

Sighs which are from lovers blown
Do but gently heave the heart:
Ev'n the tears they shed alone
Cure, like trickling balm, their smart:
Lovers, when they lose their breath,
Bleed away in easy death.

NASCENT LOVE

Love and Time with reverence use,
Treat them like a parting friend;
Nor the golden gifts refuse
Which in youth sincere they send:
For each year their price is more,
And they less simple than before.

Love, like spring-tides full and high,
Swells in every youthful vein;
But each tide does less supply,
Till they quite shrink in again:
If a flow in age appear,
'Tis but rain, and runs not clear.

John Dryden (1631–1700)

Desire

   For giving me Desire,
An Eager Thirst, a burning Ardent fire,
   A virgin Infant Flame,
A Love with which into the World I came,
   An Inward Hidden Heavenly Love,
   Which in my Soul did Work and move,
   And ever ever me Enflame,
With restlesse longing Heavenly Avarice,
   That never could be satisfied,
That did incessantly a Paradice
Unknown suggest, and som thing undescribed
   Discern, and bear me to it; be
   Thy Name for ever praisd by me…

Thomas Traherne (1637–74)

Tell Me, My Heart, if this be Love

When Delia on the plain appears,
Awed by a thousand tender fears
I would approach, but dare not move:
Tell me, my heart, if this be love?

Whene'er she speaks, my ravish'd ear
No other voice than hers can hear,
No other wit but hers approve:
Tell me, my heart, if this be love?

If she some other youth commend,
Though I was once his fondest friend,
His instant enemy I prove:
Tell me, my heart, if this be love?

When she is absent, I no more
Delight in all that pleased before–
The clearest spring, or shadiest grove:
Tell me, my heart, if this be love?

When fond of power, of beauty vain,
Her nets she spread for every swain,
I strove to hate, but vainly strove:
Tell me, my heart, if this be love?

Lord George Lyttelton (1709–73)

The Presence of Love

And in Life's noisiest hour,
There whispers still the ceaseless Love of Thee,
The heart's Self-solace and soliloquy.

You mould my Hopes, you fashion me within;
And to the leading Love-throb in the Heart
Thro' all my Being, thro' my pulses beat;
You lie in all my many Thoughts, like Light,
Like the fair light of Dawn, or summer Eve
On rippling Stream, or cloud-reflecting Lake.
And looking to the Heaven, that bends above you,
How oft! I bless the Lot, that made me love you.

Samuel Taylor Coleridge (1772–1834)

Love's Philosophy

The fountains mingle with the river
And the rivers with the ocean,
The winds of heaven mix for ever
With a sweet emotion;
Nothing in the world is single,
All things by a law divine
In one another's being mingle–
Why not I with thine?

See the mountains kiss high heaven,
And the waves clasp one another;
No sister-flower would be forgiven
If it disdain'd its brother;
And the sunlight clasps the earth,
And the moonbeams kiss the sea–
What are all these kissings worth,
If thou kiss not me?

Percy Bysshe Shelley (1792–1822)

But were I Loved

But were I loved, as I desire to be,
What is there in the great sphere of the earth,
And range of evil between death and birth,
That I should fear, if I were loved by thee?
All the inner, all the outer world of pain
Clear Love would pierce and cleave, if thou wert mine,
As I have heard that, somewhere in the main,

NASCENT LOVE

Fresh-water springs come up through bitter brine.
'Twere joy, not fear, clasped hand-in-hand with thee,
To wait for death—mute—careless of all ills,
Apart upon a mountain, tho' the surge
Of some new deluge from a thousand hills
Flung leagues of roaring foam into the gorge
Below us, as far on as eye could see.

Alfred Lord Tennyson (1809–92)

Do I Love Thee?

Do I love thee? Ask the bee
If she loves the flowery lea,
Where the honeysuckle blows
And the fragrant clover grows.
As she answers, Yes or No,
Darling! take my answer so.

Do I love thee? Ask the bird
When her matin song is heard,
If she loves the sky so fair,
Fleecy cloud and liquid air.
As she answers, Yes, or No,
Darling! take my answer so.

Do I love thee? Ask the flower
If she loves the vernal shower,
Or the kisses of the sun,
Or the dew, when day is done.
As she answers, Yes or No,
Darling! take my answer so.

John Godfrey Saxe (1816–87)

My Queen of Dreams

In the warm flushed heart of the rose-red west,
When the great sun quivered and died today,
You pulsed, O star, by yon pine-clad crest—
And throbbed till the bright eve ashened grey—
Then I saw you swim
By the shadowy rim
Where the grey gum dips to the western plain,
And you rayed delight
As you winged your flight
To the mystic spheres where your kinsmen reign.

O star, did you see her? My queen of dreams!
Was it you that glimmered the night we strayed
A month ago by these scented streams?
Half-checked by the litter the musk-buds made?
Did you sleep or wake?
Ah, for Love's sweet sake
(Though the world should fail and the soft stars wane!)
I shall dream delight
Till our souls take flight
To the mystic spheres where your kinsmen reign!

Philip Joseph Holdsworth (1849–1902)

The Kiss

Before you kissed me only winds of heaven
Had kissed me, and the tenderness of rain
Now you have come, how can I care for kisses
Like theirs again?

I sought the sea, she sent her winds to meet me,
They surged about me singing of the south
I turned my head away to keep still holy
Your kiss upon my mouth.

And swift sweet rains of shining April weather
Found not my lips where living kisses are;
I bowed my head lest they put out my glory
As rain puts out a star.

I am my love's and he is mine forever,
Sealed with a seal and safe forevermore
Think you that I could let a beggar enter
Where a king stood before?

Sara Teasdale (1884–1933)

Extract from In Memory

Serene and beautiful and very wise,
Most erudite in curious Grecian lore,
You lay and read your learned books, and bore
A weight of unshed tears and silent sighs.
The song within your heart could never rise
Until love bade it spread its wings and soar.
Nor could you look on Beauty's face before
A poet's burning mouth had touched your eyes…

Alfred Joyce Kilmer (1886–1918)

Secret Flowers

Is love a light for me? A steady light,
A lamp within whose pallid pool I dream
Over old love-books? Or is it a gleam,
A lantern coming towards me from afar
Down a dark mountain? Is my love a star?
Ah me!– so high above so coldly bright!
The fire dances. Is my love a fire
Leaping down the twilight muddy and bold?
Nay, I'd be frightened of him. I'm too cold
For quick and eager loving. There's a gold
Sheen on these flower petals as they fold
More truly mine, more like to my desire.
The flower petals fold. They are by the sun
Forgotten. In a shadowy wood they grow
Where the dark trees keep up a to-and-fro
Shadowy waving. Who will watch them shine
When I have dreamed my dream? Ah, darling mine,
Find them, gather them for me one by one.

Katherine Mansfield (1888–1923)

49

CELEBRATION
AND DEVOTION

If One Chaste Love

If one chaste love, if one divine compassion,
If one destiny is equal for two lovers,
If one hard fate of the one is felt by the other,
If one spirit, if one will guides two hearts;
If one soul in two bodies makes itself eternal,
Lifting both to heaven with a single wing,
If Love in one blow and one golden arrow
The hearts in two chests can burn and tear;
If the one loves the other and neither loves himself,
With one pleasure and one delight, to such a measure
That one and the other desire to reach a single end:
Thousands and thousands would not make a hundredth
Of such a knot of love, or of such a faith:
And only anger could break and untie it.

Michelangelo Buonarroti (1475–1564)

Sonnet 18

Shall I compare thee to a summer's day?
Thou art more lovely and more temperate:
Rough winds do shake the darling buds of May,
And summer's lease hath all too short a date:
Sometime too hot the eye of heaven shines,
And often is his gold complexion dimm'd;
And every fair from fair sometime declines,
By chance, or nature's changing course untrimm'd;
But thy eternal summer shall not fade,
Nor lose possession of that fair thou ow'st,
Nor shall death brag thou wander'st in his shade,
When in eternal lines to time thou grow'st;
So long as men can breathe, or eyes can see,
So long lives this, and this gives life to thee.

William Shakespeare (1564–1616)

Extract from Othello Act 2 Scene I

It gives me wonder great as my content
To see you here before me. O my soul's joy!
If after every tempest come such calms,
May the winds blow till they have waken'd death,
And let the labouring bark climb hills of seas
Olympus-high and duck again as low
As hell's from heaven. If it were now to die,
'Twere now to be most happy; for fear
My soul hath her content so absolute
That not another comfort like to this
Succeeds in unknown fate.

William Shakespeare (1564–1616)

That Time and Absence Proves

Absence, hear thou my protestation
Against thy strength,
Distance and length:
Do what thou canst for alteration,
For hearts of truest mettle
Absence doth join and Time doth settle.

Who loves a mistress of such quality,
His mind hath found
Affection's ground
Beyond time, place, and all mortality.
To hearts that cannot vary
Absence is present, Time doth tarry.

My senses want their outward motion
Which now within
Reason doth win,
Redoubled by her secret notion:
Like rich men that take pleasure
In hiding more than handling treasure.

By Absence this good means I gain,
That I can catch her
Where none can watch her,
In some close corner of my brain:
There I embrace and kiss her,
And so enjoy her and none miss her.

John Donne (1572–1631)

Love Not Me

Love not me for comely grace,
For my pleasing eye or face,

Nor for any outward part:
No, nor for a constant heart!
For these may fail or turn to ill:
Should thou and I sever.

Keep, therefore, a true woman's eye,
And love me still, but know not why!
So hast thou the same reason still
To dote upon me ever.

John Wilbye (1574–1638)

To Anthea, who may command him anything

Bid me to live, and I will live
Thy Protestant to be;
Or bid me love, and I will give
A loving heart to thee.

A heart as soft, a heart as kind,
A heart as sound and free,
As in the whole world thou canst find,
That heart I'll give to thee.

Bid that heart stay, and it will stay,
To honour thy decree;
Or bid it languish quite away,
And't shall do so for thee.

Bid me to weep, and I will weep
While I have eyes to see;
And having none, yet I will keep
A heart to weep for thee.

Bid me despair, and I'll despair
Under that cypress-tree;
Or bid me die, and I will dare
E'en death to die for thee.

Thou art my life, my love, my heart,
The very eyes of me;
And hast command of every part
To live and die for thee.

Robert Herrick (1591–1674)

Mediocrity in Love Rejected

Give me more Love, or more Disdain;
The Torrid, or the Frozen Zone
Bring equall ease unto my paine;
The Temperate affords me none:
Either extreme, of Love, or Hate,
Is sweeter than a calme estate.

Give me a storme; if it be Love,
Like Danae in that golden showre
I swim in pleasure; if it prove
Disdain, that Torrent will devour
My Vulture-hopes; and he's possest
Of Heaven, that's but from Hell releast:
Then crown my joyes, or cure my pain;
Give me more Love, or more Disdain.

Thomas Carew (1595–1640)

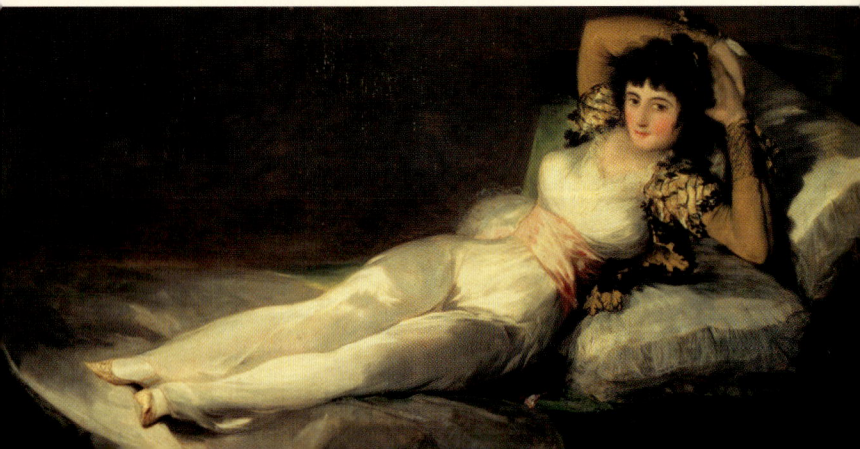

The Lover's Clock

That none beguiled be by Time's quick flowing,
Lovers have in their hearts a clock still going;
For, though Time be nimble, his motions
Are quicker
Are thicker
Where Love hath his notions.

Hope is the mainspring on which moves desire,
And these do the less wheels, fear, joy, inspire;
The balance is thought, evermore
Clicking
And striking,
And ne'er giving o'er.

Occasion's the hand which still's moving round,
Till by it the critical hour may be found;
And, when that falls out, it will strike
Kisses,
Strange blisses,
And what you best like.

Sir John Suckling (1609–42)

Out Upon it, I Have Loved

Out upon it! I have loved
Three whole days together;
And am like to love three more,
If it prove fair weather.

Time shall moult away his wings
Ere he shall discover
In the whole wide world again
Such a constant lover.

But the spite on't is, no praise
Is due at all to me:
Love with me had made no stays
Had it any been but she.

Had it any been but she,
And that very face,
There had been at least ere this
A dozen dozen in her place.

Sir John Suckling (1609–42)

The Symptoms of Love

Would my Delia know if I love, let her take
My last thought at night, and the first when I wake;
With my prayers and best wishes preferred for her sake.

Let her guess what I muse on, when rambling alone
I stride o'er the stubble each day with my gun,
Never ready to shoot till the covey is flown.

Let her think what odd whimsies I have in my brain,
When I read one page over and over again,
And discover at last that I read it in vain.

Let her say why so fixed and so steady my look,
Without ever regarding the person who spoke,
Still affecting to laugh, without hearing the joke.

Or why when the pleasure her praises I hear,
(That sweetest of melody sure to my ear),
I attend, and at once inattentive appear.

And lastly, when summoned to drink to my flame,
Let her guess why I never once mention her name,
Though herself and the woman I love are the same.

William Cowper (1731–1800)

Perfect Woman

She was a phantom of delight
When first she gleam'd upon my sight;
A lovely apparition, sent
To be a moment's ornament;
Her eyes as stars of twilight fair;
Like twilight's, too, her dusky hair;
But all things else about her drawn
From May-time and the cheerful dawn;
A dancing shape, an image gay,
To haunt, to startle, and waylay.

I saw her upon nearer view,
A Spirit, yet a Woman too!
Her household motions light and free,
And steps of virgin liberty;
A countenance in which did meet
Sweet records, promises as sweet;
A creature not too bright or good
For human nature's daily food;
For transient sorrows, simple wiles,
Praise, blame, love, kisses, tears, and smiles.

And now I see with eye serene
The very pulse of the machine;
A being breathing thoughtful breath,
A traveller between life and death;
The reason firm, the temperate will,

Endurance, foresight, strength, and skill;
A perfect Woman, nobly plann'd,
To warm, to comfort, and command;
And yet a Spirit still, and bright
With something of angelic light.

William Wordsworth (1770–1850)

Love

In peace, Love tunes the shepherd's reed;
In war, he mounts the warrior's steed;
In halls, in gay attire is seen;
In hamlets, dances on the green.
Love rules the court, the camp, the grove,
And men below and saints above;
For love is heaven, and heaven is love.

Sir Walter Scott (1771–1832)

Genevieve

Maid of my love! sweet Genevieve!
In beauty's light you glide along;
Your eye is like the star of eve,
And sweet your voice, as seraph's song.
Yet not your heavenly beauty gives
This heart with passion soft to glow:
Within your soul a voice there lives!
It bids you hear the tale of woe.
When sinking low the suff'rer wan
Beholds no hand outstretched to save,
Fair, as the bosom of the swan
That rises graceful o'er the wave,
I've seen your breast with pity heave
And therefore love I you, sweet Genevieve!

Samuel Taylor Coleridge (1772–1834)

She Walks in Beauty

She walks in beauty, like the night
Of cloudless climes and starry skies;
And all that's best of dark and bright
Meet in her aspect and her eyes:
Thus mellow'd to that tender light
Which heaven to gaudy day denies.
One shade the more, one ray the less,
Had half impair'd the nameless grace
Which waves in every raven tress,
Or softly lightens o'er her face;
Where thoughts serenely sweet express
How pure, how dear their dwelling-place.

And on that cheek, and o'er that brow,
So soft, so calm, yet eloquent,
The smiles that win, the tints that glow,
But tell of days in goodness spent,
A mind at peace with all below,
A heart whose love is innocent!

George Gordon, Lord Byron (1788–1824)

To Harriet

Thy look of love has power to calm
The stormiest passion of my soul;
Thy gentle words are drops of balm
In life's too bitter bowl;
No grief is mine, but that alone
These choicest blessings I have known.

Harriet! if all who long to live
In the warm sunshine of thine eye,
That price beyond all pain must give,—
Beneath thy scorn to die;
Then hear thy chosen own too late
His heart most worthy of thy hate.

Be thou, then, one among mankind
Whose heart is harder not for state,
Thou only virtuous, gentle, kind,

Amid a world of hate;
And by a slight endurance seal
A fellow-being's lasting weal.

For pale with anguish is his cheek,
His breath comes fast, his eyes are dim,
Thy name is struggling ere he speak,
Weak is each trembling limb;
In mercy let him not endure
The misery of a fatal cure.

Oh, trust for once no erring guide!
Bid the remorseless feeling flee;
'Tis malice, 'tis revenge, 'tis pride,
'Tis anything but thee;
Oh, deign a nobler pride to prove,
And pity if thou canst not love.

Percy Bysshe Shelley (1792–1822)

I Love Thee

I love thee, as I love the calm
Of sweet, star-lighted hours!
I love thee, as I love the balm
Of early jes'mine flow'rs.
I love thee, as I love the last
Rich smile of fading day,
Which lingereth, like the look we cast,
On rapture pass'd away.
I love thee as I love the tone
Of some soft-breathing flute
Whose soul is wak'd for me alone,
When all beside is mute.

I love thee as I love the first
Young violet of the spring;
Or the pale lily, April-nurs'd,
To scented blossoming.
I love thee, as I love the full,
Clear gushings of the song,
Which lonely, sad and beautiful–
At night-fall floats along,
Pour'd by the bulbul forth to greet
The hours of rest and dew;
When melody and moonlight meet
To blend their charm, and hue.
I love thee, as the glad bird loves
The freedom of its wing,
On which delightedly it moves
In wildest wandering.

I love thee as I love the swell,
And hush, of some low strain,
Which bringeth, by its gentle spell,
The past to life again.
Such is the feeling which from thee
Nought earthly can allure:
'Tis ever link'd to all I see
Of gifted, high and pure!

Eliza Acton (1799–1859)

A Woman's Last Word

Let's contend no more, Love,
Strive nor weep:
All be as before, Love,
Only sleep!

What so wild as words are?
I and thou
In debate, as birds are,
Hawk on bough!

See the creature stalking
While we speak!
Hush and hide the talking,
Cheek on cheek!

What so false as truth is,
False to thee?
Where the serpent's tooth is
Shun the tree—

Where the apple reddens
Never pry—
Lest we lose our Edens,
Eve and I.

Be a god and hold me
With a charm!
Be a man and fold me
With thine arm!

Teach me, only teach, Love
As I ought
I will speak thy speech, Love,
Think thy thought—

Meet, if thou require it,
Both demands,
Laying flesh and spirit
In thy hands.

That shall be to-morrow
Not to-night:
I must bury sorrow
Out of sight:

Must a little weep, Love,
(Foolish me!)
And so fall asleep, Love,
Loved by thee.

Robert Browning (1812–89)

Beautiful Dreamer

Beautiful dreamer, wake unto me,
Starlight and dewdrops are waiting for thee;
Sounds of the rude world heard in the day,
Lull'd by the moonlight have all pass'd a way!

Beautiful dreamer, queen of my song,
List while I woo thee with soft melody;
Gone are the cares of life's busy throng,
Beautiful dreamer, awake unto me!

Beautiful dreamer, out on the sea
Mermaids are chaunting the wild lorelie;
Over the streamlet vapors are borne,
Waiting to fade at the bright coming morn.

Beautiful dreamer, beam on my heart,
E'en as the morn on the streamlet and sea;
Then will all clouds of sorrow depart,
Beautiful dreamer, awake unto me!

Stephen Foster (1826–64)

Love-sweetness

Sweet dimness of her loosened hair's downfall
About thy face; her sweet hands round thy head
In gracious fostering union garlanded;
Her tremulous smiles; her glances' sweet recall
Of love; her murmuring sighs memorial;

Her mouth's culled sweetness by thy kisses shed
On cheeks and neck and eyelids, and so led
Back to her mouth, which answers there for all:—
What sweeter than these things, except the thing
In lacking which all these would lose their sweet:—

The confident heart's still fervor: the swift beat
And soft subsidence of the spirit's wing,
Then when it feels, in cloud-girt wayfaring,
The breath of kindred plumes against its feet?

Dante Gabriel Rossetti (1828–82)

My Queen

He loves not well whose love is bold!
I would not have thee come too nigh:
The sun's gold would not seem pure gold
Unless the sun were in the sky;
To take him thence and chain him near
Would make his beauty disappear.

He keeps his state,—keep thou in thine,
And shine upon me from afar!
So shall I bask in light divine,
That falls from love's own guiding star;
So shall thy eminence be high,
And so my passion shall not die.

But all my life shall reach its hands
Of lofty longing toward thy face,
And be as one who speechless stands
In rapture at some perfect grace!
My love, my hope, my all shall be
To look to heaven and look to thee!

Thy eyes shall be the heavenly lights;
Thy voice the gentle summer breeze,
What time it sways, on moonlit nights,
The murmuring tops of leafy trees;
And I shall touch thy beauteous form
In June's red roses, rich and warm.

But thou thyself shalt come not down
From that pure region far above;
But keep thy throne and wear thy crown,
Queen of my heart and queen of love!
A monarch in thy realm complete,
And I a monarch—at thy feet!

William Winter (1836–1917)

Cleone

Sing her a song of the sun:
Fill it with tones of the stream,
Echoes of waters that run
Glad with the gladdening gleam.
Let it be sweeter than rain,
Lit by a tropical moon:
Light in the words of the strain,
Love in the ways of the tune.
Softer than seasons of sleep:
Dearer than life at its best!
Give her a ballad to keep,
Wove of the passionate West:
Give it and say of the hours
'Haunted and hallowed of thee,
Flower-like woman of flowers,
What shall the end of them be?'

You that have loved her so much,
Loved her asleep and awake,
Trembled because of her touch,
What have you said for her sake?
Far in the falls of the day,
Down in the meadows of myrrh,
What has she left you to say
Filled with the beauty of her?

Take her the best of your thoughts,
Let them be gentle and grave,
Say, 'I have come to thy courts,

Maiden, with all that I have.'
So she may turn with her sweet
Face to your love and to you,
Learning the way to repeat
Words that are brighter than dew.

Henry Kendall (1839–82)

My Heart Shall be Thy Garden

My heart shall be thy garden. Come, my own,
Into thy garden; thine be happy hours
Among my fairest thoughts, my tallest flowers,
From root to crowning petal, thine alone.
Thine is the place from where the seeds are sown
Up to the sky inclosed, with all its showers.
But ah, the birds, the birds! Who shall build bowers
To keep these thine? O friend, the birds have flown.

For as these come and go, and quit our pine
To follow the sweet season, or new-comers,
Sing one song only from our alder-trees,
My heart has thoughts, which, though thine eyes hold mine.
Flit to the silent world and other summers,
With wings that dip beyond the silver seas.

Alice Meynell (1847–1922)

What are you, Love?

What are you, love? A flame from heaven?
A radiant smile are you?
The heaven has not your eyes' bright gleams,
The heaven has not their blue.

The rose has not your snowy breast;
In the moon's face we seek
In vain the rosy flush that dyes
Your soft and blushing cheek.

By night you smile upon the stars,
And on the amorous moon,
By day upon the waves, the flowers -
Why not on one alone?

But, though I pray to you with tears,
With tears and bitter sighs,
You will not deign me yet one glance
Cast by your shining eyes.

O love, are you a mortal maid,
Or angel formed of light?
The spring rose and the radiant moon
Envy your beauty bright;

And when your sweet and thrilling voice
Is heard upon the air,
In cypress depths the nightingale
Is silent in despair.

Would I, a zephyr, might caress
Your bright brow's dreams in sleep,
Breathe gently on your lips, and dry
Your tears, if you should weep!

Or would that in your garden fair
A weeping rose I grew;
And when you came resplendent there
At morning with the dew,

I'd give fresh colour to your cheek
That makes the rose look pale,
Shed on your breast my dew, and there
My latest breath exhale.

Oh, would I were a limpid brook!
If softly you drew nigh,
And smiled into my mirror clear,
My blue waves would run dry.

Oh, would I were a sunbeam bright,
To make you seem more fair,
Touching your face, and dying soon
Amid your fragrant hair!

But, if you love another,
His gravestone may I be!
Then you would linger near me,
Your tears would fall on me;
Your sighs would wander o'er me,
Sighs for his early doom.
To touch you, O beloved,
I must become a tomb!

Bedros Tourian (1851–72)

Happiest

Calling you now, not for your flesh I call,
Nor for the mad, long raptures of the night
And passion in its beauty and its might,
When the ecstatic bodies rise and fall.
I cannot feign: God knows I see it all—
The flaming senses, raving with delight,
The leopards, swift and terrible and white,
Within the loins that shudder as they crawl.

All that could I exultingly forego,
Could I but stand, one flash of time, and see
Your heavenly, entrancing face, and know
I stood most blest of all beneath the sun,
Hearing these words from your fond lips to me:
'I love, love you, and love no other one!'

George Sterling (1869–1926)

The Beloved: Reflections on the Path of the Heart

Tell me, O people, tell me!
Who among you would not wake from
the sleep of life
if love were to brush your spirit with its fingertips?

Who among you would not forsake your
father and your mother
and your home if the girl whom
your heart loved were to call to him?

Who among you would not cross the
seas, traverse deserts,
go over mountains and valleys to reach
the woman whom his spirit has chosen?

What youth would not follow his heart to
the ends of the earth
to breathe the sweetness of his lover's breath,
feel the soft touch of her hands,
delight in the melody of her voice?

What man would not immolate his soul
that its smoke might rise to a god who
would hear his plea
and answer his prayer?

Khalil Gibran (1883–1931)

I Would Live in Your Love

I would live in your love as the sea-grasses live in the sea,
Borne up by each wave as it passes,
drawn down by each wave that recedes;
I would empty my soul as the dreams
that have gathered in me,
I would beat with your heart as it beats,
I would follow your soul as it leads.

Sara Teasdale (1884–1933)

FULFILLED LOVE

Sonnet 116

Let me not to the marriage of true minds
Admit impediments. Love is not love
Which alters when it alteration finds,
Or bends with the remover to remove:
O, no! it is an ever-fixed mark,
That looks on tempests and is never shaken;
It is the star to every wandering bark,
Whose worth's unknown, although his height be taken.
Love's not Time's fool, though rosy lips and cheeks
Within his bending sickle's compass come;
Love alters not with his brief hours and weeks,
But bears it out even to the edge of doom.
If this be error, and upon me prov'd,
I never writ, nor no man ever lov'd.

William Shakespeare (1564–1616)

Air and Angels

Twice or thrice had I loved thee,
Before I knew thy face or name;
So in a voice, so in a shapeless flame,
Angels affect us oft, and worshipped be;
   Still when, to where thou wert, I came,
Some lovely glorious nothing I did see,
   But since my soul, whose child love is,
Takes limbs of flesh, and else could nothing do,
   More subtle than the parent is
Love must not be, but take a body too,
   And therefore what thou wert, and who
   I bid love ask, and now
That it assume thy body, I allow,
And fix itself in thy lip, eye, and brow

Whilst thus to ballast love, I thought,
And so more steadily to have gone,
With wares which would sink admiration,
I saw, I had love's pinnace overfraught,
   Every thy hair for love to work upon
Is too much, some fitter must be sought;
   For, nor in nothing, nor in things
Extreme, and scatt'ring bright, can love inhere;
   Then as an angel, face and wings
Of air, not pure as it, yet doth wear,
   So thy love may be my love's sphere;
   Just such disparity
As is 'twixt air and angels' purity
'Twixt women's love, and men's will ever be.

John Donne (1572–1631)

A Nymph's Passion

I love, and he loves me again,
Yet dare I not tell who;
For if the nymphs should know my swain,
I fear they'd love him too;
Yet if he be not known,
The pleasure is as good as none,
For that's a narrow joy is but our own.

I'll tell, that if they be not glad,
They may not envy me;
But then if I grow jealous mad
And of them pitied be,
It were a plague 'bove scorn;
And yet it cannot be forborne
Unless my heart would, as my thought, be torn.

He is, if they can find him, fair
And fresh, and fragrant too,
As summer's sky or purgéd air,
And looks as lilies do
That are this morning blown:
Yet, yet I doubt he is not known,
And fear much more that more of him be shown.

But he hath eyes so round and bright,
As make away my doubt,
Where Love may all his torches light,
Though Hate had put them out;
But then t' increase my fears

FULFILLED LOVE

What nymph soe'er his voice but hears
Will be my rival, though she have but ears.

I'll tell no more, and yet I love,
And he loves me; yet no one
Unbecoming thought doth move
From either heart I know:
But so exempt from blame
As it would be to each a fame,
If love or fear would let me tell his name

Benjamin Jonson (1572–1637)

All for Love

O talk not to me of a name great in story;
The days of our youth are the days of our glory;
And the myrtle and ivy of sweet two-and-twenty
Are worth all your laurels, though ever so plenty.

What are garlands and crowns to the brow that is wrinkled?
'Tis but as a dead flower with May-dew besprinkled:
Then away with all such from the head that is hoary–
What care I for the wreaths that can only give glory?

Oh Fame! –if I e'er took delight in thy praises,
'Twas less for the sake of thy high-sounding phrases,
Than to see the bright eyes of the dear one discover
She thought that I was not unworthy to love her.

There chiefly I sought thee, there only I found thee;
Her glance was the best of the rays that surround thee;
When it sparkled o'er aught that was bright in my story,
I knew it was love, and I felt it was glory.

George Gordon, Lord Byron (1788–1824)

Of Pearls and Stars

The pearly treasures of the sea,
The lights that spatter heaven above,
More precious than these wonders are
My heart-of-hearts filled with your love.

The ocean's power, the heavenly sights
Cannot outweigh a love filled heart.
And sparkling stars or glowing pearls
Pale as love flashes, beams and darts.

So, little, youthful maiden come
Into my ample, feverish heart
For heaven and earth and sea and sky
Do melt as love has melt my heart.

Heinrich Heine (1797–1856)

Wondrous Moment

The wondrous moment of our meeting
I well remember you appear
Before me like a vision fleeting,
A beauty's angel pure and clear.

In hopeless ennui surrounding
The worldly bustle, to my ear
For long your tender voice kept sounding,
For long in dreams came features dear.

Time passed. Unruly storms confounded
Old dreams, and I from year to year
Forgot how tender you had sounded,
Your heavenly features once so dear.

My backwoods days dragged slow and quiet
Dull fence around, dark vault above
Devoid of God and uninspired,
Devoid of tears, of fire, of love.

Sleep from my soul began retreating,
And here you once again appear
Before me like a vision fleeting,
A beauty's angel pure and clear.

In ecstasy the heart is beating,
Old joys for it anew revive;
Inspired and God-filled, it is greeting
The fire, and tears, and love alive.

Alexander Sergeyvich Pushkin (1799–1837)

Time of Roses

It was not in the Winter
Our loving lot was cast;
It was the time of roses—
We pluck'd them as we pass'd!

That churlish season never frown'd
On early lovers yet:
O no—the world was newly crown'd
With flowers when first we met!

'Twas twilight, and I bade you go,
But still you held me fast;
It was the time of roses—
We pluck'd them as we pass'd!

Thomas Hood (1799–1845)

Ruth

She stood breast-high amid the corn,
Clasp'd by the golden light of morn,
Like the sweetheart of the sun,
Who many a glowing kiss had won.

On her cheek an autumn flush,
Deeply ripen'd;–such a blush
In the midst of brown was born,
Like red poppies grown with corn.

Round her eyes her tresses fell,
Which were blackest none could tell,
But long lashes veil'd a light,
That had else been all too bright.

And her hat, with shady brim,
Made her tressy forehead dim;
Thus she stood amid the stooks,
Praising God with sweetest looks:–

Sure, I said, Heav'n did not mean,
Where I reap thou shouldst but glean,
Lay thy sheaf adown and come,
Share my harvest and my home.

Thomas Hood (1799–1845)

The Newly-Wedded

Now the rite is duly done,
Now the word is spoken,
And the spell has made us one
Which may ne'er be broken;
Rest we, dearest, in our home,
Roam we o'er the heather:
We shall rest, and we shall roam,
Shall we not together?

From this hour the summer rose
Sweeter breathes to charm us;
From this hour the winter snows
Lighter fall to harm us:
Fair or foul—on land or sea—
Come the wind or weather,
Best and worst, whate'er they be,
We shall share together.

Death, who friend from friend can part,
Brother rend from brother,
Shall but link us, heart and heart,
Closer to each other:
We will call his anger play,
Deem his dart a feather,
When we meet him on our way
Hand in hand together.

Winthrop Mackworth Praed (1802–1859)

The Owl and the Pussy-Cat

The Owl and the Pussy-Cat went to sea
    In a beautiful pea-green boat.
They took some honey, and plenty of money
    Wrapped up in a five-pound note.
The Owl looked up to the stars above,
    And sang to a small guitar,
'O lovely Pussy! O Pussy, my love,
What a beautiful Pussy you are,
        You are,
        You are!
What a beautiful Pussy you are!'

Pussy said to the Owl, 'You elegant fowl!
    How charmingly sweet you sing!
O let us be married! Too long we have tarried:
    But what shall we do for a ring?'
They sailed away, for a year and a day,
    To the land where the Bong-Tree grows;
And there in a wood a Piggy-wig stood,
With a ring at the end of his nose,
        His nose,
        His nose!
With a ring at the end of his nose.

'Dear Pig, are you willing to sell for one shilling
   Your ring?' Said the Piggy, 'I will.'
So they took it away, and were married next day
   By the Turkey who lives on the hill.
They dinèd on mince and slices of quince,
   Which they ate with a runcible spoon;
And hand in hand, on the edge of the sand
   They danced by the light of the moon,
     The moon,
     The moon,
They danced by the light of the moon.

Edward Lear (1812–88)

Cristina

She should never have looked at me
If she meant I should not love her!
There are plenty men, you call such,
I suppose she may discover
All her soul to, if she pleases,
And yet leave much as she found them:
But I'm not so, and she knew it
When she fixed me, glancing round them,

What? To fix me thus meant nothing?
But I can't tell (there's my weakness)
What her look said!—no vile cant, sure,
About need to strew the bleakness
Of some lone shore with its pearl-seed.
That the sea feels—no strange yearning
That such souls have, most to lavish
Where there's chance of least returning.

Oh, we're sunk enough here, God knows!
But not quite so sunk that moments,
Sure tho' seldom, are denied us,
When the spirit's true endowments
Stand out plainly from its false ones,
And apprise it if pursuing
Or the right way or the wrong way,
To its triumph or undoing.

There are flashes struck from midnights,
There are fire-flames noondays kindle,
Whereby piled-up honours perish,
Whereby swollen ambitions dwindle,
While just this or that poor impulse,
Which for once had play unstifled,
Seems the sole work of a life-time
That away the rest have trifled.

Doubt you if, in some such moment,
As she fixed me, she felt clearly,
Ages past the soul existed,
Here an age 'tis resting merely,
And hence fleets again for ages,
While the true end, sole and single,
It stops here for is, this love-way,
With some other soul to mingle?

Else it loses what it lived for,
And eternally must lose it;
Better ends may be in prospect,
Deeper blisses (if you choose it),
But this life's end and this love-bliss
Have been lost here. Doubt you whether
This she felt as, looking at me,
Mine and her souls rushed together?

Oh, observe! Of course, next moment,
The world's honours, in derision,
Trampled out the light for ever:
Never fear but there's provision
Of the devil's to quench knowledge
Lest we walk the earth in rapture!
Making those who catch God's secret
Just so much more prize their capture!

Such am I: the secret's mine now!
She has lost me, I have gained her;
Her soul's mine: and thus, grown perfect,
I shall pass my life's remainder.
Life will just hold out the proving
Both our powers, alone and blended:
And then, come next life quickly!
This world's use will have been ended.

Robert Browning (1812–1889)

I Loved Her that She was Beautiful

I loved her for that she was beautiful;
And that to me she seem'd to be all Nature,
And all varieties of things in one:
Would set at night in clouds of tears, and rise
All light and laughter in the morning; fear
No petty customs nor appearances;
But think what others only dream'd about;
And say what others did but think; and do
What others dared not do: so pure withal
In soul; in heart and act such conscious yet
Such perfect innocence, she made round her
A halo of delight. 'Twas these which won me;
And that she never school'd within her breast
One thought or feeling, but gave holiday
To all; and that she made all even mine
In the communion of love: and we
Grew like each other, for we loved each other;
She, mild and generous as the air in spring;
And I, like earth all budding out with love.

Philip James Bailey (1816–1902)

Wild Nights

Wild nights! Wild nights!
Were I with thee,
Wild nights should be
Our luxury!

Futile the winds
To a heart in port,–
Done with the compass,
Done with the chart.

Rowing in Eden!
Ah! the sea!
Might I but moor
To-night in thee!

Emily Dickinson (1830–86)

A Birthday

My heart is like a singing bird
Whose nest is in a water'd shoot;
My heart is like an apple-tree
Whose boughs are bent with thick-set fruit;
My heart is like a rainbow shell
That paddles in a halcyon sea;
My heart is gladder than all these,
Because my love is come to me.

Raise me a daïs of silk and down;
Hang it with vair and purple dyes;
Carve it in doves and pomegranates,
And peacocks with a hundred eyes;
Work it in gold and silver grapes,
In leaves and silver fleurs-de-lys;
Because the birthday of my life
Is come, my love is come to me

Christina Georgina Rossetti (1830–94)

Last

Friend, whose smile has come to be
Very precious unto me,
Though I know I drank not first
Of your love's bright fountain-burst,
Yet I grieve not for the past,
So you only love me last!

Other souls may find their joy
In the blind love of a boy:
Give me that which years have tried,
Disciplined and purified,—
Such as, braving sun and blast,
You will bring to me at last!

There are brows more fair than mine,
Eyes of more bewitching shine,
Other hearts more fit, in truth,

FULFILLED LOVE

For the passion of your youth;
But, their transient empire past,
You will surely love me last!

Wing away your summer-time,
Find a love in every clime,
Roam in liberty and light,—
I shall never stay your flight;
For I know, when all is past
You will come to me at last!

Change and flutter as you will,
I shall smile securely still;
Patiently I trust and wait
Though you tarry long and late;
Prize your spring till it be past,
Only, only love me last!

Elizabeth Allen Akers (1832–1911)

At Last

At last, when all the summer shine
That warmed life's early hours is past,
Your loving fingers seek for mine
And hold them close—at last—at last!
Not oft the robin comes to build
Its nest upon the leafless bough
By autumn robbed, by winter chilled,—
But you, dear heart, you love me now.

Though there are shadows on my brow
And furrows on my cheek, in truth,—
The marks where Time's remorseless plough
Broke up the blooming sward of Youth,—
Though fled is every girlish grace
Might win or hold a lover's vow,
Despite my sad and faded face,
And darkened heart, you love me now!

I count no more my wasted tears;
They left no echo of their fall;
I mourn no more my lonesome years;
This blessed hour atones for all.
I fear not all that Time or Fate
May bring to burden heart or brow,—
Strong in the love that came so late,
Our souls shall keep it always now!

Elizabeth Allen Akers (1832–1911)

Love is Enough

Love is enough: though the World be a-waning,
And the woods have no voice but the voice of complaining,
Though the sky be too dark for dim eyes to discover
The gold-cups and daisies fair blooming thereunder,
Though the hills be held shadows, and the sea a dark wonder,
And this day draw a veil over all deeds pass'd over,
Yet their hands shall not tremble, their feet shall not falter;
The void shall not weary, the fear shall not alter
These lips and these eyes of the loved and the lover.

William Morris (1834–96)

An Old Sweetheart of Mine

As one who cons at evening o'er an album all alone,
And muses on the faces of the friends that he has known,
So I turn the leaves of Fancy, till in shadowy design
I find the smiling features of an old sweetheart of mine.

The lamplight seems to glimmer with a flicker of surprise,
As I turn it low, to rest me of the dazzle in my eyes,
And light my pipe in silence, save a sigh that seems to yoke
Its fate with my tobacco, and to vanish with the smoke.

'Tis a fragrant retrospection, for the loving thoughts that start
Into being are like perfumes from the blossom of the heart;
And to dream the old dreams over is a luxury divine–
When my truant fancies wander with that old sweetheart of mine.

Though I hear, beneath my study, like a fluttering of wings,
The voices of my children and the mother as she sings,
I feel no twinge of conscience to deny me any theme
When Care has cast her anchor in the harbor of a dream.

In fact, to speak in earnest, I believe it adds a charm
To spice the good a trifle with a little dust of harm;
For I find an extra flavor in Memory's mellow wine
That makes me drink the deeper to that old sweetheart of mine.

A face of lily-beauty, with a form of airy grace,
Floats out of my tobacco as the genii from the vase;
And I thrill beneath the glances of a pair of azure eyes,
As glowing as the summer and as tender as the skies.

I can see the pink sunbonnet and the little checkered dress
She wore when first I kissed her, and she answered the caress
With the written declaration that, 'as surely as the vine
Grew round the stump,' she loved me,—that old sweetheart of mine!

And again I feel the pressure of her slender little hand,
As we used to talk together of the future we had planned:
When I should be a poet, and with nothing else to do
But write the tender verses that she set the music to;

When we should live together in a cozy little cot,
Hid in a nest of roses, with a fairy garden-spot,
Where the vines were ever fruited, and the weather ever fine,
And the birds were ever singing for that old sweetheart of mine;

And I should be her lover forever and a day,
And she my faithful sweetheart till the golden hair was gray;
And we should be so happy that when either's lips were dumb
They would not smile in heaven till the other's kiss had come.

But ah! my dream is broken by a step upon the stair,
And the door is softly opened, and my wife is standing there!
Yet with eagerness and rapture all my visions I resign
To greet the living presence of that old sweetheart of mine

James Whitcomb Riley (1849–1916)

A Valentine to My Wife

Accept, dear girl, this little token,
And if between the lines you seek,
You' the love I've often spoken–
The love my dying lips shall speak.

Our little ones are making merry
O'er am'rous ditties rhymed in jest,
But in these words (though awkward–very)
The genuine article's expressed.

You are as fair and sweet and tender,
Dear brown-eyed little sweetheart mine,
As when, a callow youth and slender,
I asked to be your Valentine.

What though these years of ours be fleeting?
What though the years of youth be flown?
I'll mock old Tempus with repeating,
'I love my love and her alone!'

And when I fall before his reaping,
And when my stuttering speech is dumb,
Think not my love is dead or sleeping,
But that it waits for you to come.

So take, dear love, this little token,
And if there speaks in any line
The sentiment I'd fain have spoken,
Say, will you kiss your Valentine?

Eugene Field (1850–95)

Love

Love is the sunlight of the soul,
That, shining on the silken-tressèd head
Of her we love, around it seems to shed
A golden angel-aureole.

And all her ways seem sweeter ways
Than those of other women in that light:
She has no portion with the pallid night,
But is a part of all fair days.

Joy goes where she goes, and good dreams—
Her smile is tender as an old romance
Of Love that dies not, and her soft eye's glance
Like sunshine set to music seems.

Queen of our fate is she, but crowned
With purple hearts-ease for her womanhood.
There is no place so poor where she has stood
But evermore is holy ground.

An angel from the heaven above
Would not be fair to us as she is fair:
She holds us in a mesh of silken hair,
This one sweet woman whom we love.

We pray thee, Love, our souls to steep
In dreams wherein thy myrtle flowereth;
So when the rose leaves shiver, feeling Death
Pass by, we may remain asleep:

Asleep, with poppies in our hands,
From all the world and all its cares apart—
Cheek close to cheek, heart beating against heart,
While through Life's sandglass run the sands

Victor James Daley (1858–1905)

A Golden Day

I found you and I lost you,
All on a gleaming day.
The day was filled with sunshine,
And the land was full of May.
A golden bird was singing
Its melody divine,
I found you and I loved you,
And all the world was mine.
I found you and I lost you,
All on a golden day,
But when I dream of you, dear,
It is always brimming May.

Paul Laurence Dunbar (1872–1906)

Time and Again

Time and again, however well we know the landscape of love,
and the little church-yard with lamenting names,
and the frightfully silent ravine wherein all the others end:
time and again we go out two together,
under the old trees, lie down again and again
between the flowers, face to face with the sky.

Rainer Maria Rilke (1875–1926)

After You Speak

After you speak
And what you meant
Is plain,
My eyes
Meet yours that mean,
With your cheeks and hair,
Something more wise,
More dark,
And far different.
Even so the lark
Loves dust
And nestles in it
The minute
Before he must
Soar in lone flight
So far,
Like a black star
He seems—
A mote
Of singing dust
Afloat
Above,
The dreams
And sheds no light.
I know your lust
Is love.

Edward Thomas (1878–1917)

On the Balcony

In front of the sombre mountains, a faint, lost ribbon of rainbows;
And between us and it, the thunder;
And down below in the green wheat, the labourers
Stand like dark stumps, still in the green wheat

You are near to me, and your naked feet in their sandals,
And through the scent of the balcony's naked timber
I distinguish the scent of your hair: so now the limber
Lightning falls from heaven.

Adown the pale-green glacier river floats
A dark boat through the gloom—and whither.
The thunder roars. But still we have each other!
And disappear—what have we but each other?
The boat has gone.

D.H. Lawrence (1885–1930)

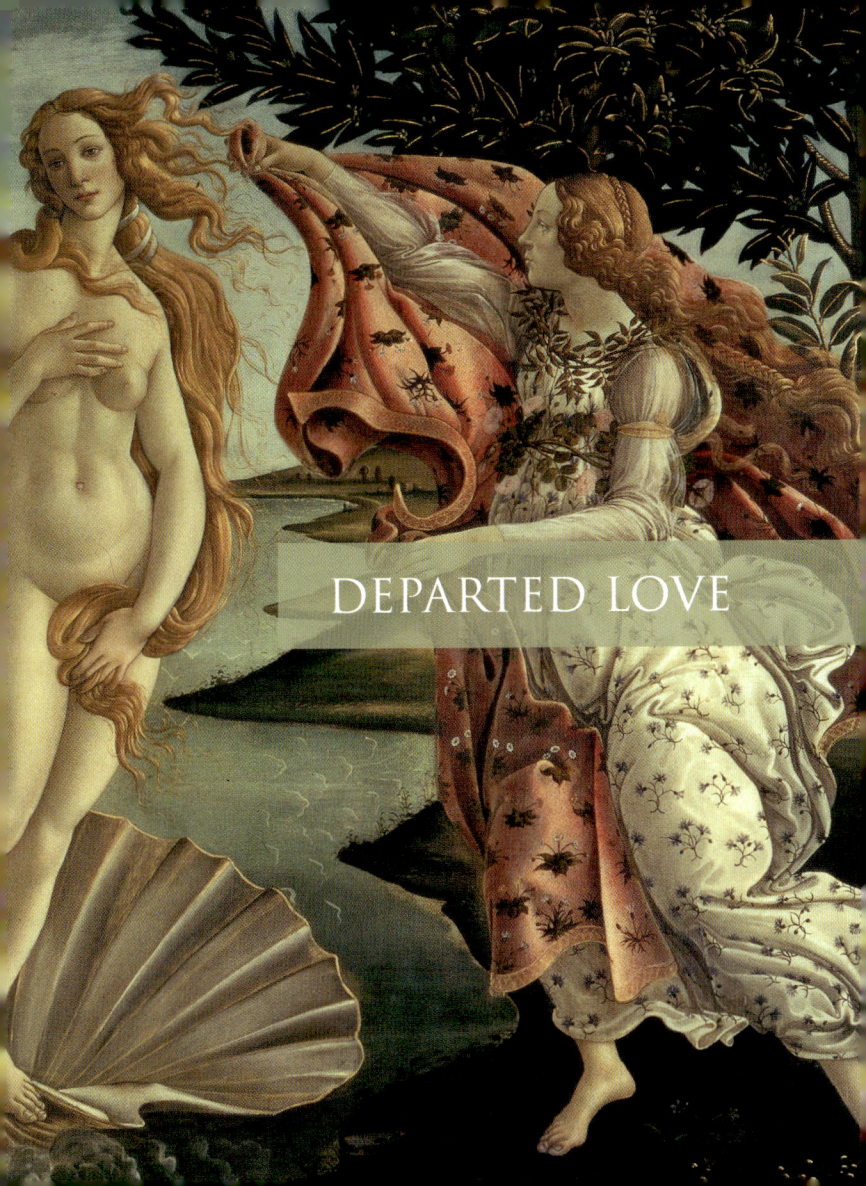

DEPARTED LOVE

To Althea from Prison

When Love with unconfinèd wings
Hovers within my gates,
And my divine Althea brings
To whisper at the grates;
When I lie tangled in her hair
And fetter'd to her eye,
The birds that wanton in the air
Know no such liberty.

When flowing cups run swiftly round
With no allaying Thames,
Our careless heads with roses crown'd,
Our hearts with loyal flames;
When thirsty grief in wine we steep,
When healths and draughts go free—
Fishes that tipple in the deep
Know no such liberty.

DEPARTED LOVE

When, linnet-like confinèd,
I with shriller throat shall sing
The sweetness, mercy, majesty
And glories of my King;
When I shall voice aloud how good
He is, how great should be,
Enlargèd winds, that curl the flood,
Know no such liberty.

Stone walls do not a prison make,
Nor iron bars a cage;
Minds innocent and quiet take
That for an hermitage;
If I have freedom in my love
And in my soul am free,
Angels alone, that soar above,
Enjoy such liberty.

Colonel Richard Lovelace (1618–57)

To Lucasta, Going beyond the Seas

If to be absent were to be
Away from thee;
Or that when I am gone
You or I were alone;
Then, my Lucasta, might I crave
Pity from blustering wind or swallowing wave.

Though seas and land betwixt us both,
Our faith and troth,
Like separated souls,
All time and space controls:
Above the highest sphere we meet
Unseen, unknown, and greet as Angels greet.

So then we do anticipate
Our after-fate,
And are alive i' the skies,
If thus our lips and eyes
Can speak like spirits unconfined
In Heaven, their earthy bodies left behind.

Colonel Richard Lovelace (1618–57)

A Red, Red Rose

Tune: Major Graham

O my luve's like a red, red rose
That's newly sprung in June;
O my luve's like the melodie
That's sweetly play'd in tune.

As fair thou art, my bonnie lass,
So deep in luve am I,
And I will luve thee still, my Dear,
Till a' the seas gang dry.

Till a' the seas gang dry, my Dear,
And the rocks melt wi' the sun:
I will luve thee still my Dear,
While the sands o' life shall run.

And fare thee weel, my only Luve,
And fare thee weel a while!
And I will come again, my Luve,
Tho' it were ten thousand mile!

Robert Burns (1759–96)

Fair Ines

O saw ye not fair Ines?
She's gone into the West,
To dazzle when the sun is down,
And rob the world of rest:
She took our daylight with her,
The smiles that we love best,
With morning blushes on her cheek,
And pearls upon her breast.

O turn again, fair Ines,
Before the fall of night,
For fear the Moon should shine alone,
And stars unrivall'd bright;
And blessèd will the lover be
That walks beneath their light,
And breathes the love against thy cheek
I dare not even write!

Would I had been, fair Ines,
That gallant cavalier,
Who rode so gaily by thy side,
And whisper'd thee so near!
Were there no bonny dames at home,
Or no true lovers here,
That he should cross the seas to win
The dearest of the dear?

DEPARTED LOVE

I saw thee, lovely Ines,
Descend along the shore,
With bands of noble gentlemen,
And banners waved before;
And gentle youth and maidens gay,
And snowy plumes they wore:
It would have been a beauteous dream,–
If it had been no more!

Alas, alas! fair Ines,
She went away with song,
With Music waiting on her steps,
And shoutings of the throng;
But some were sad, and felt no mirth,
But only Music's wrong,
In sounds that sang Farewell, farewell
To her you've loved so long.

Farewell, farewell, fair Ines!
That vessel never bore
So fair a lady on its deck,
Nor danced so light before,–
Alas for pleasure on the sea,
And sorrow on the shore!
The smile that bless'd one lover's heart
Has broken many more!

Thomas Hood (1799–1845)

Give all to Love

Give all to love;
Obey thy heart;
Friends, kindred, days,
Estate, good fame,
Plans, credit, and the muse;
Nothing refuse.

'Tis a brave master,
Let it have scope,
Follow it utterly,
Hope beyond hope;
High and more high,
It dives into noon,
With wing unspent,
Untold intent;
But 'tis a god,
Knows its own path,
And the outlets of the sky.
'Tis not for the mean,
It requireth courage stout,
Souls above doubt,
Valor unbending;
Such 'twill reward,
They shall return
More than they were,
And ever ascending.

DEPARTED LOVE

Leave all for love;—
Yet, hear me, yet,
One word more thy heart behoved,
One pulse more of firm endeavor,
Keep thee to-day,
To-morrow, for ever,
Free as an Arab
Of thy beloved.
Cling with life to the maid;
But when the surprise,
Vague shadow of surmise,
Flits across her bosom young
Of a joy apart from thee,
Free be she, fancy-free,
Do not thou detain a hem,
Nor the palest rose she flung
From her summer diadem

Though thou loved her as thyself,
As a self of purer clay,
Tho' her parting dims the day,
Stealing grace from all alive,
Heartily know,
When half-gods go,
The gods arrive.

Ralph Waldo Emerson (1803–82)

I do not Love Thee

I do not love thee!—no! I do not love thee!
And yet when thou art absent I am sad;
And envy even the bright blue sky above thee,
Whose quiet stars may see thee and be glad.

I do not love thee!—yet, I know not why,
Whate'er thou dost seems still well done, to me:
And often in my solitude I sigh
That those I do love are not more like thee!

I do not love thee!—yet, when thou art gone,
I hate the sound (though those who speak be dear)
Which breaks the lingering echo of the tone
Thy voice of music leaves upon my ear.

I do not love thee!—yet thy speaking eyes,
With their deep, bright, and most expressive blue,
Between me and the midnight heaven arise,
Oftener than any eyes I ever knew.

I know I do not love thee! yet, alas!
Others will scarcely trust my candid heart;
And oft I catch them smiling as they pass,
Because they see me gazing where thou art.

Caroline Elizabeth Sarah Norton (1808–77)

Annabel Lee

It was many and many a year ago,
In a kingdom by the sea,
That a maiden there lived whom you may know
By the name of Annabel Lee;
And this maiden she lived with no other thought
Than to love and be loved by me.

I was a child and she was a child,
In this kingdom by the sea;
But we loved with a love that was more than love
I and my Annabel Lee;
With a love that the winged seraphs of heaven
Coveted her and me.

And this was the reason, that long ago,
In this kingdom by the sea,
A wind blew out of a cloud, chilling
My beautiful Annabel Lee;
So that her high-born kinsman came
And bore her away from me,
To shut her up in a sepulchre,
In this kingdom by the sea.

The angel, not half so happy in heaven,
Went envying her and me...
Yes! that was the reason (as all men know,
In this kingdom by the sea)
That the wind came out of the cloud by night,
Chilling and killing my Annabel Lee.

But our love it was stronger by far than the love
Of those who were older than we,
Of many far wiser than we
And neither the angels in heaven above,
Nor the demons down under the sea,
Can ever dissever my soul from the soul
Of the beautiful Annabel Lee,

For the moon never beams, without bringing me dreams
Of the beautiful Annabel Lee;
And the stars never rise, but I feel the bright eyes
Of the beautiful Annabel Lee;
And so, all the night-tide, I lie down by the side
Of my darling, my darling, my life and my bride,
In the sepulchre there by the sea,
In her tomb by the sounding sea.

Edgar Allan Poe (1809-49)

A Dream within a Dream

Take this kiss upon the brow!
And, in parting from you now,
Thus much let me avow–
You are not wrong, who deem
That my days have been a dream;
Yet if hope has flown away
In a night, or in a day,
In a vision, or in none,
Is it therefore the less gone?
All that we see or seem
Is but a dream within a dream.

I stand amid the roar
Of a surf-tormented shore,
And I hold within my hand
Grains of the golden sand–
How few! yet how they creep
Through my fingers to the deep,
While I weep while I weep!
O God! can I not grasp
Them with a tighter clasp?
O God! can I not save
One from the pitiless wave?
Is all that we see or seem
But a dream within a dream?

Edgar Allan Poe (1809–49)

You and I

My hand is lonely for your clasping, dear;
My ear is tired waiting for your call.
I want your strength to help, your laugh to cheer;
Heart, soul and senses need you, one and all.
I droop without your full, frank sympathy;
We ought to be together you and I;
We want each other so, to comprehend
The dream, the hope, things planned, or seen, or wrought.
Companion, comforter and guide and friend,
As much as love asks love, does thought ask thought.
Life is so short, so fast the lone hours fly,
We ought to be together, you and I.

Henry Alford (1810–71)

Parting

There's no use in weeping,
Though we are condemned to part:
There's such a thing as keeping
A remembrance in one's heart:

There's such a thing as dwelling
On the thought ourselves have nurs'd,
And with scorn and courage telling
The world to do its worst.

We'll not let its follies grieve us,
We'll just take them as they come;
And then every day will leave us
A merry laugh for home.

When we've left each friend and brother,
When we're parted wide and far,
We will think of one another,
As even better than we are.

Every glorious sight above us,
Every pleasant sight beneath,
We'll connect with those that love us,
Whom we truly love till death!

In the evening, when we're sitting
By the fire perchance alone,
Then shall heart with warm heart meeting,
Give responsive tone for tone.

DEPARTED LOVE

We can burst the bonds which chain us,
Which cold human hands have wrought,
And where none shall dare restrain us
We can meet again, in thought.

So there's no use in weeping,
Bear a cheerful spirit still;
Never doubt that Fate is keeping
Future good for present ill!

Charlotte Brontë (1816–55)

Good-Bye My Fancy

Good-bye my Fancy!
Farewell dear mate, dear love!
I'm going away, I know not where,
Or to what fortune, or whether I may ever see you again,
So Good-bye my Fancy.
Now for my last—let me look back a moment;
The slower fainter ticking of the clock is in me,
Exit, nightfall, and soon the heart-thud stopping.
Long have we lived, joy'd, caress'd together;
Delightful! now separation—Good-bye my Fancy.
Yet let me not be too hasty,
Long indeed have we lived, slept, filter'd, become really
blended into one;
Then if we die we die together, (yes, we'll remain one,)
If we go anywhere we'll be better off and blither, and learn
something,
Maybe it is yourself now really ushering me
to the true songs, (who knows?)
Maybe it is you the mortal knob really undoing, turning
—so now finally,
Good-bye and hail! my Fancy!

Walt Whitman (1819–92)

Weep Not Too Much

Weep not too much, my darling;
Sigh not too oft for me;
Say not the face of Nature
Has lost its charm for thee.
I have enough of anguish
In my own breast alone;
Thou canst not ease the burden, Love,
By adding still thine own.
I know the faith and fervour
Of that true heart of thine;
But I would have it hopeful
As thou wouldst render mine.
At night, when I lie waking,
More soothing it will be
To say 'She slumbers calmly now,'
Than say 'She weeps for me.'

When through the prison grating
The holy moonbeams shine,
And I am wildly longing
To see the orb divine
Not crossed, deformed, and sullied
By those relentless bars
That will not show the crescent moon,
And scarce the twinkling stars,

It is my only comfort
To think, that unto thee
The sight is not forbidden–
The face of heaven is free.
If I could think Zerona
Is gazing upward now–
Is gazing with a tearless eye
A calm unruffled brow;

That moon upon her spirit
Sheds sweet, celestial balm,–
The thought, like Angel's whisper,
My misery would calm.
And when, at early morning,
A faint flush comes to me,
Reflected from those glowing skies
I almost weep to see;

Or when I catch the murmur
Of gently swaying trees,
Or hear the louder swelling
Of the soul-inspiring breeze,
And pant to feel its freshness
Upon my burning brow,
Or sigh to see the twinkling leaf,
And watch the waving bough;

If, from these fruitless yearnings
Thou wouldst deliver me,
Say that the charms of Nature
Are lovely still to thee;
While I am thus repining,
O! let me but believe,
'These pleasures are not lost to her,'
And I will cease to grieve.

O, scorn not Nature's bounties!
My soul partakes with thee.
Drink bliss from all her fountains,
Drink for thyself and me!
Say not, 'My soul is buried
In dungeon gloom with thine;'
But say, 'His heart is here with me;
His spirit drinks with mine.'

Anne Brontë (1820–49)

To an Absent Lover

That so much change should come when thou dost go,
Is mystery that I cannot ravel quite.
The very house seems dark as when the light
Of lamps goes out. Each wonted thing doth grow
So altered, that I wander to and fro
Bewildered by the most familiar sight,
And feel like one who rouses in the night
From dream of ecstasy, and cannot know
At first if he be sleeping or awake.
My foolish heart so foolish for thy sake
Hath grown, dear one!
Teach me to be more wise.
I blush for all my foolishness doth lack;
I fear to seem a coward in thine eyes.
Teach me, dear one,—but first thou must come back!

Helen Hunt Jackson (1830–85)

Forgiven

I dreamed so dear a dream of you last night!
I thought you came. I was so glad, so gay,
I whispered, 'Those were foolish words to say;
I meant them not. I cannot bear the sight
Of your dear face. I cannot meet the light
Of your dear eyes upon me. Sit, I pray—
Sit here beside me; turn your look away,
And lay your cheek on mine,'Till morning bright
We sat so, and we did not speak. I knew
All was forgiven, so nestled there
With your arms round. Swift the sweet hours flew.
At last I waked, and sought you everywhere.
How long, dear, think you, that my glad cheek will
Burn as it burns with our cheek's pressure still?

Helen Hunt Jackson (1830–85)

Thalia

I say it under the rose—
Oh, thanks!—yes, under the laurel,
We part lovers, not foes;
We are not going to quarrel.

We have too long been friends
On foot and in gilded coaches,
Now that the whole thing ends,
To spoil our kiss with reproaches.

I leave you; my soul is wrung;
I pause, look back from the portal—
Ah, I no more am young,
And you, child, you are immortal!

Mine is the glacier's way,
Yours is the blossom's weather—
When were December and May
Known to be happy together?

Before my kisses grow tame,
Before my moodiness grieve you,
While yet my heart is flame,
And I all lover, I leave you.

So, in the coming time,
When you count the rich years over,
Think of me in my prime,
And not as a white-haired lover,

DEPARTED LOVE

Fretful, pierced with regret,
The wraith of a dead Desire,
Thrumming a cracked spinet
By a slowly dying fire.

When, at last, I am cold–
Years hence, if the gods so will it–
Say, 'He was true as gold,'
And wear a rose in your fillet!

Others, tender as I,
Will come and sue for caresses,
Woo you, win you, and die–
Mind you, a rose in your tresses!

Some Melpomene woo,
Some hold Clio the nearest;
You, sweet Comedy,–you
Were ever sweetest and dearest!

Nay, it is time to go.
When writing your tragic sister
Say to that child of woe
How sorry I was I missed her.

Really, I cannot stay,
Though 'parting is such sweet sorrow'
Perhaps I will, on my way
Down-town, look in to-morrow!

Thomas Bailey Aldrich (1836–1907)

Dear Love, Good-Night

Dear love, good-night. And, tender sleep,
Seal up her lids like these drowsed flowers,
To make day fair when they unclose.
Be hushed around her, Night, and keep
Thy silent guard on her repose;
But speed thine hours.

Dear love, sleep on. This weary space
I wake and long for day and thee,
And count the slow stars from their west.
Sleep while I hunger for thy face,
Sleep, dearest, in unbroken rest;
But dream of me.

Augusta Davies Webster (1837–94)

The Girl I Left Behind Me

With sweet Regret – the dearest thing that Yesterday has left us–
We often turn our homeless eyes to scenes whence Fate has reft us.
Here sitting by a fading flame, wild waifs of song remind me
Of Annie with her gentle ways, the Girl I left behind me.

I stood beside the surging sea, with lips of silent passion–
I faced you by the surging sea, O brows of mild repression!
I never said – 'my darling, stay!' – the moments seemed to bind me
To something stifling all my words for the Girl I left behind me.

The pathos worn by common things – by every wayside flower,
Or Autumn leaf on lonely winds, revives the parting hour.
Ye swooning thoughts without a voice – ye tears which rose to blind me,
Why did she fade into the Dark, the Girl I left behind me.

At night they always come to me, the tender and true-hearted;
And in my dreams we join again the hands which now are parted;
And, looking through the gates of Sleep, the pleasant Moon doth find me
For ever wandering with my Love, the Girl I left behind me.

You know my life is incomplete, O far-off faint ideal!
When shall I reach you from a depth of darkness which is real?
So I may mingle, soul in soul, with her that Heaven assigned me;
So she may lean upon my love, the Girl I left behind me.

Henry Kendall (1839–82)

Love Unexpressed

The sweetest notes among the human
  heart-strings are dull with rust;
The sweetest chords, adjusted by the angels,
  are clogged with dust;
We pipe and pipe again our dreary music
  upon the self-same strains,
While sounds of crime, and fear, and
  desolation, come back in sad refrains.

On through the world we go, an army
  marching with listening ears,
Each longing, sighing, for the heavenly
  music he never hears;
Each longing, sighing, for a word of comfort,
  a word of tender praise,
A word of love, to cheer the endless journey
  of Earth's hard, busy days.

They love us, and we know it; this suffices
  for reason's share.
Why should they pause to give that love
  expression with gentle care?
Why should they pause? But still our hearts
  are aching with all the gnawing pain
Of hungry love that longs to hear the music,
  and longs and longs in vain.

DEPARTED LOVE

We love them, and they know it; if we falter,
  with fingers numb,
Among the unused strings of love's
  expression, the notes are dumb.
We shrink within ourselves in voiceless
  sorrow, leaving the words unsaid,
And, side by side with those we love the
  dearest, in silence on we tread.

Thus on we tread, and thus each heart
  in silence its fate fulfils,
Waiting and hoping for the heavenly
  music beyond the distant hills.
The only difference of the love in heaven
  from love on earth below is:
Here we love and know not how to tell it,
  and there we all shall know.

Constance Fenimore Woolson (1840–94)

Are You Loving Enough?

Are you loving enough? There is some one dear,
Some one you hold as the dearest of all
In the holiest shrine of your heart.
Are you making it known? Is the truth of it clear
To the one you love? If death's quick call
Should suddenly tear you apart,
Leaving no time for a long farewell,
Would you feel you had nothing to tell–
Nothing you wished you had said before
The closing of that dark door?

Are you loving enough? The swift years fly–
Oh, faster and faster they hurry away,
And each one carries its dead.
The good deed left for the by and by,
The word to be uttered another day,
May never be done or said.
Let the love word sound in the listening ear,
Nor wait to speak it above a bier.
Oh the time for telling your love is brief,
But long, long, long is the time for grief.
Are you loving enough?

Ella Wheeler Wilcox (1850–1919)

195

Friendship After Love

After the fierce midsummer all ablaze
Has burned itself to ashes, and expires
In the intensity of its own fires,
There come the mellow, mild, St. Martin days
Crowned with the calm of peace, but sad with haze.
So after Love has led us, till he tires
Of his own throes, and torments, and desires,
Comes large-eyed friendship: with a restful gaze,
He beckons us to follow, and across
Cool verdant vales we wander free from care.
Is it a touch of frost lies in the air?
Why are we haunted with a sense of loss?
We do not wish the pain back, or the heat;
And yet, and yet, these days are incomplete.

Ella Wheeler Wilcox (1850–1919)

A Dream

My dead love came to me, and said:
'God gives me one hour's rest,
To spend with thee on earth again:
How shall we spend it best?'

'Why, as of old,' I said; and so
We quarrelled, as of old:
But, when I turned to make my peace,
That one short hour was told.

Stephen Phillips (1864–1915)

Beloved, Lost to Begin With

Beloved,
lost to begin with, never greeted,
I do not know what tones most please you.
No more when the future's wave hangs poised is it you
I try to discern there. All the greatest
images in me, far-off experienced landscape,
towers and towns and bridges and un-
suspected turns of the way,
and the power of those lands once intertwined
with the life of the gods:
mount up within me to mean
you, who forever elude.

Oh, you are the gardens!
Oh, with such yearning
hope I watched them! An open window
in a country house, and you almost stepped out
thoughtfully to meet me. Streets I discovered,–
you had just walked down them,
and sometimes in dealers' shops the mirrors,
Still dizzy with you, returned with a start
my too-sudden image. Who knows whether the
self-same bird didn't ring through each of us,
separately, yesterday evening?

Rainer Maria Rilke (1875–1926)

Longing for Love

Neither the issue nor the sire,
neither fulfillment nor desire
am I for anyone,
am I for anyone.
I am as all men, the sunless sea,
the alien thule, mystery,
a fleeing wisp of light,
a fleeing wisp of light.
But I must look for friends and brothers;
I want to show myself to others
that seeing they will see,
that seeing they will see.
For this my lyric masochism;
I long to close the gaping schism,
and thus belong somewhere,
and thus belong somewhere.

Endre Ady (1877–1919)

The Gift

What can I give you, my lord, my lover,
You who have given the world to me,
Showed me the light and the joy that cover
The wild sweet earth and the restless sea?
All that I have are gifts for your giving–
If I gave them again, you would find them old,
And your soul would weary of always living
Before the mirror my life would hold.
What shall I give you, my lord, my lover?
The gift that breaks the heart in me:
I bid you awake at dawn and discover
I have gone my way and left you free.

Sara Teasdale (1884–1933)

A Love Song

Reject me not if I should say to you
I do forget the sounding of your voice,
I do forget your eyes that searching through
The mists perceive our marriage, and rejoice.

Yet, when the apple-blossom opens wide
Under the pallid moonlight's fingering,
I see your blanched face at my breast, and hide
My eyes from diligent work, malingering.

Ah, then, upon my bedroom I do draw
The blind to hide the garden, where the moon
Enjoys the open blossoms as they straw
Their beauty for his taking, boon for boon.

And I do lift my aching arms to you,
And I do lift my anguished, avid breast,
And I do weep for very pain of you,
And fling myself at the doors of sleep, for rest.

And I do toss through the troubled night for you,
Dreaming your yielded mouth is given to mine,
Feeling your strong breast carry me on into
The peace where sleep is stronger even than wine.

D. H. Lawrence (1885–1930)

BEWARE LOVE

The Appeal

And wilt thou leave me thus!
Say nay, say nay, for shame!
To save thee from the blame
Of all my grief and grame.
And wilt thou leave me thus?
Say nay! say nay!

And wilt thou leave me thus,
That hath loved thee so long
In wealth and woe among:
And is thy heart so strong
As for to leave me thus?
Say nay! say nay!

And wilt thou leave me thus,
That hath given thee my heart
Never for to depart
Neither for pain nor smart:
And wilt thou leave me thus?
Say nay! say nay!

And wilt thou leave me thus,
And have no more pitye
Of him that loveth thee?
Alas, thy cruelty!
And wilt thou leave me thus?
Say nay! say nay!

Sir Thomas Wyatt (1503–42)

On Monsieur's Departure

I grieve and dare not show my discontent,
I love and yet am forced to seem to hate,
I do, yet dare not say I ever meant,
I seem stark mute but inwardly to prate.
I am and not, I freeze and yet am burned.
Since from myself another self I turned.

My care is like my shadow in the sun,
Follows me flying, flies when I pursue it,
Stands and lies by me, doth what I have done.
His too familiar care doth make me rue it.
No means I find to rid him from my breast,
Till by the end of things it be supprest.

Some gentler passion slide into my mind,
For I am soft and made of melting snow;
Or be more cruel, love, and so be kind.
Let me or float or sink, be high or low.
Or let me live with some more sweet content,
Or die and so forget what love ere meant.

Queen Elizabeth I (1533–1603)

My Love is like to Ice

My love is like to ice, and I to fire:
How comes it then that this her cold so great
Is not dissolved through my so hot desire,
But harder grows the more I her entreat?
Or how comes it that my exceeding heat
Is not allayed by her heart-frozen cold,
But that I burn much more in boiling sweat,
And feel my flames augmented manifold?
What more miraculous thing may be told,
That fire, which all things melts, should harden ice,
And ice, which is congeal'd with senseless cold,
Should kindle fire by wonderful device?
Such is the power of love in gentle mind,
That it can alter all the course of kind.

Edmund Spenser (1552–99)

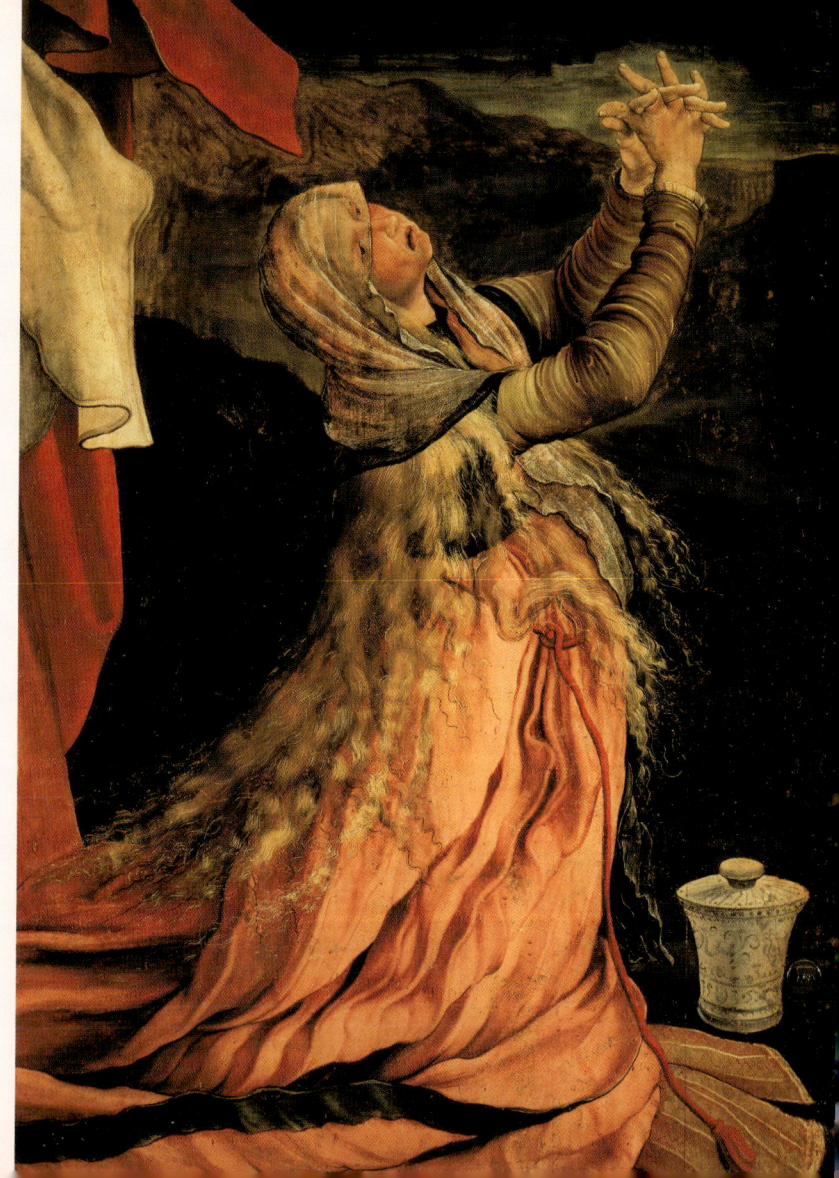

Love is a Sickness

Love is a sickness full of woes,
All remedies refusing;
A plant that with most cutting grows,
Most barren with best using.
Why so?

More we enjoy it, more it dies;
If not enjoy'd, it sighing cries–
Heigh ho!

Love is a torment of the mind,
A tempest everlasting;
And Jove hath made it of a kind
Not well, nor full nor fasting.
Why so?

More we enjoy it, more it dies;
If not enjoy'd, it sighing cries–
Heigh ho!

Samuel Daniel (1562–1619)

Love's Farewell

Since there's no help, come let us kiss and part,–
Nay I have done, you get no more of me;
And I am glad, yea, glad with all my heart,
That thus so cleanly I myself can free;
Shake hands for ever, cancel all our vows,
And when we meet at any time again,
Be it not seen in either of our brows
That we one jot of former love retain.
Now at the last gasp of love's latest breath,
When his pulse failing, passion speechless lies,
When faith is kneeling by his bed of death,
And innocence is closing up his eyes,
–Now if thou would'st, when all have given him over,
From death to life thou might'st him yet recover!

Michael Drayton (1563–1631)

Sonnet 137

Thou blind fool, Love, what dost thou to mine eyes
That they behold, and see not what they see?
They know what beauty is, see where it lies,
Yet what the best is take the worst to be.
If eyes, corrupt by over-partial looks,
Be anchor'd in the bay where all men ride,
Why of eyes' falsehood hast thou forged hooks,
Whereto the judgment of my heart is tied?
Why should, my heart think that a several plot,
Which my heart knows the wide world's common place?
Or mine eyes, seeing this, say this is not,
To put fair truth upon so foul a face?
In things right true my heart and eyes have erred,
And to this false plague are they now transferred.

William Shakespeare (1564–1616)

Take, Oh Take Those Lips Away

Take, oh take those lips away,
That so sweetly were forsworn,
And those eyes, the break of day,
Lights that do mislead the morn:
But my kisses bring again,
Seals of love, but sealed in vain.

Hide, oh hide those hills of snow,
Which thy frozen bosom bears,
On whose tops the pinks that grow
Are yet of those that April wears.
But first set my poor heart free,
Bound in those icy chains by thee.

John Fletcher (1579–1625)

To Oenone

What conscience, say, is it in thee,
When I a heart had one,
To take away that heart from me,
And to retain thy own?

For shame or pity now incline
To play a loving part;
Either to send me kindly thine,
Or give me back my heart.

Covet not both; but if thou dost
Resolve to part with neither,
Why, yet to show that thou art just,
Take me and mine together!

Robert Herrick (1591–1674)

The Godhead fires

I Prithee Send Me Back My Heart

I prithee send me back my heart,
Since I cannot have thine;
For if from yours you will not part,
Why then shouldst thou have mine?

Yet now I think on't, let it lie,
To find it were in vain;
For thou'st a thief in either eye
Would steal it back again.

Why should two hearts in one breast lie,
And yet not lodge together?
O love, where is thy sympathy,
If thus our breasts thou sever?

But love is such a mystery,
I cannot find it out;
For when I think I'm best resolved,
I then am most in doubt.

Then farewell care, and farewell woe,
I will no longer pine;
For I'll believe I have her heart
As much as she hath mine.

Sir John Suckling (1609–42)

Song

Love in fantastic triumph sate
Whilst bleeding hearts around him flow'd,
For whom fresh pains he did create
And strange tyrannic power he show'd:
From thy bright eyes he took his fires,
Which round about in sport he hurl'd;
But 'twas from mine he took desires
Enough t' undo the amorous world.

From me he took his sighs and tears,
From thee his pride and cruelty;
From me his languishments and fears,
And every killing dart from thee.
Thus thou and I the god have arm'd
But my poor heart alone is harm'd,
Whilst thine the victor is, and free!

Aphra Behn (1640–89)

A Woman to Her Lover

Do you come to me to bend me to your will
as conqueror to the vanquished
to make of me a bondslave
to bear you children, wearing out my life
in drudgery and silence
no servant will I be
if that be what you ask. O lover I refuse you!

Or if you think to wed with one from heaven sent
whose every deed and word and wish is golden
a wingless angel who can do no wrong, go!
I am no doll to dress and sit for feeble worship
if that be what you ask, fool, I refuse you!

Or if you think in me to find
a creature who will have no greater joy
than gratify your clamorous desire,
my skin soft only for your fond caresses
my body supple only for your sense delight.
Oh shame, and pity and abasement.
Not for you the hand of any wakened woman of our time.

But lover, if you ask of me
that I shall be your comrade, friend, and mate,
to live and work, to love and die with you,
that so together we may know the purity and height
of passion, and of joy and sorrow,
then o husband, I am yours forever

and our co-equal love will make the stars to laugh with joy
and to its circling fugue pass, hand holding hand
until we reach the very heart of god.

Christina Walsh (1750–1800)

The Garden of Love

I laid me down upon a bank,
Where Love lay sleeping;
I heard among the rushes dank
Weeping, weeping.

Then I went to the heath and the wild,
To the thistles and thorns of the waste;
And they told me how they were beguiled,
Driven out, and compelled to the chaste.

I went to the Garden of Love,
And saw what I never had seen;

BEWARE LOVE

A Chapel was built in the midst,
Where I used to play on the green.

And the gates of this Chapel were shut
And 'Thou shalt not,' writ over the door;
So I turned to the Garden of Love
That so many sweet flowers bore.

And I saw it was filled with graves,
And tombstones where flowers should be;
And priests in black gowns were walking their rounds,
And binding with briars my joys and desires.

William Blake (1757–1827)

Love in the Guise of Friendship

Talk not of love, it gives me pain,
For love has been my foe;
He bound me in an iron chain,
And plung'd me deep in woe.

But friendship's pure and lasting joys,
My heart was form'd to prove;
There, welcome win and wear the prize,
But never talk of love.

Your friendship much can make me blest,
O why that bliss destroy?
Why urge the only, one request
You know I will deny?

Your thought, if Love must harbor there,
Conceal it in that thought;
Nor cause me from my bosom tear
The very friend I sought.

Robert Burns (1759–96)

Love's Last Adieu

The roses of love glad the garden of life,
Though nurtured 'mid weeds dropping pestilent dew,
Till time crops the leaves with unmerciful knife,
Or prunes them for ever, in love's last adieu!

In vain, with endearments, we soothe the sad heart,
In vain do we vow for an age to be true;
The chance of an hour may command us to part,
Or death disunite us in love's last adieu!

Still Hope, breathing peace, through the grief-swollen breast,
Will whisper, 'Our meeting we yet may renew:'
With this dream of deceit, half our sorrow's represt,
Nor taste we the poison, of love's last adieu!

Oh! mark you yon pair: in the sunshine of youth,
Love twined round their childhood his flowers as they grew;
They flourish awhile, in the season of truth,
Till chill'd by the winter of love's last adieu!

Sweet lady! why thus doth a tear steal its way,
Down a cheek which outrivals thy bosom in hue?
Yet why do I ask? to distraction a prey,
Thy reason has perish'd with love's last adieu!

Oh! who is yon misanthrope, shunning mankind?
From cities to caves of the forest he flew:

There, raving, he howls his complaint to the wind,
The mountains reverberate love's last adieu!

Now hate rules a heart which in love's easy chains,
Once passion's tumultuous blandishments knew;
Despair now inflames the dark tide of his veins;
He ponders in frenzy on love's last adieu!

How he envies the wretch with a soul wrapt in steel!
His pleasures are scarce, yet his troubles are few,
Who laughs at the pang that he never can feel,
And dreads not the anguish of love's last adieu!

Youth flies, life decays, even hope is o'ercast;
No more, with love's former devotion, we sue:
He spreads his young wing, he retires with the blast;
The shroud of affection is love's last adieu!

In this life of probation, for rapture divine,
Astrea declares that some penance is due;
From him, who has worshipp'd at love's gentle shrine,
The atonement is ample in love's last adieu!

Who kneels to the god, on his altar of light
Must myrtle and cypress alternately strew:
His myrtle, an emblem of purest delight,
His cypress, the garland of love's last adieu!

Gordon George, Lord Byron (1788–1824)

First Love

I ne'er was struck before that hour
With love so sudden and so sweet,
Her face it bloomed like a sweet flower
And stole my heart away complete.
My face turned pale as deadly pale.
My legs refused to walk away,
And when she looked, what could I ail?
My life and all seemed turned to clay.

And then my blood rushed to my face
And took my eyesight quite away,
The trees and bushes round the place
Seemed midnight at noonday.
I could not see a single thing,
Words from my eyes did start–
They spoke as chords do from the string,
And blood burnt round my heart.

Are flowers the winter's choice?
Is love's bed always snow?
She seemed to hear my silent voice,
Not love's appeals to know.
I never saw so sweet a face
As that I stood before.
My heart has left its dwelling-place
And can return no more

John Clare (1793–1864)

La Belle Dame Sans Merci

O what can ail thee, knight-at-arms,
  Alone and palely loitering?
The sedge has withered from the lake,
  And no birds sing.

O what can ail thee, knight-at-arms,
  So haggard and so woe-begone?
The squirrel's granary is full,
  And the harvest's done.

I see a lily on thy brow
  With anguish moist and fever-dew;
And on thy cheeks a fading rose
  Fast withereth too.

I met a lady in the meads,
  Full beautiful—a faery's child,
Her hair was long, her foot was light,
  And her eyes were wild.

I made a garland for her head,
  And bracelets too, and fragrant zone;
She looked at me as she did love,
  And made sweet moan.

I set her on my pacing steed,
  And nothing else saw all day long;
For sideways would she lean, and sing
  A faery's song.

She found me roots of relish sweet,
    And honey wild and manna-dew,
And sure in language strange she said—
    'I love thee true.'

She took me to her elfin grot,
    And there she wept and sigh'd full sore,
And there I shut her wild, wild eyes
    With kisses four.

And there she lulled me asleep,
    And there I dream'd–ah! woe betide!
The latest dream I ever dream'd
    On the cold hill side.
I saw pale kings and princes too,
    Pale warriors, death-pale were they all;
Who cried, 'La belle Dame sans Merci
    Hath thee in thrall!

I saw their starved lips in the gloam
    With horrid warning gaped wide,
And I awoke and found me here
    On the cold hill's side.

And this is why I sojourn here
    Alone and palely loitering,
Though the sedge is withered from the lake,
    And no birds sing.

John Keats (1795–1821)

Revenge

I would not, in the wildness of revenge,
Give poison to mine enemy, nor strike
My dagger to his heart, but I would plant
Love, burning, hopeless and unquenchable–
Within the inmost foldings of his breast,
And bid him die the dark, and ling'ring death,
Of the pale victims, who expire beneath
The pow'r of that deep passion. Earth can show
No bitterness like this! The shroud of thought
Which gathers round them, gloomy as the grave;
The wasting, but unpitied pangs, which wear
The frame away, and make the tortur'd mind
Almost a chaos in its agony;

The writhings of the spirit, doom'd to see
A rival bless'd; and utter, cold, despair:
These are its torments! Are they not enough
To satisfy the most remorseless hate?

Eliza Acton (1799–1859)

Forgiveness

My heart was heavy, for its trust had been
Abused, its kindness answered with foul wrong;
So, turning gloomily from my fellow-men,
One summer Sabbath day I strolled among
The green mounds of the village burial-place;
Where, pondering how all human love and hate
Find one sad level; and how, soon or late,
Wronged and wrongdoer, each with meekened face,
And cold hands folded over a still heart,
Pass the green threshold of our common grave,
Whither all footsteps tend, whence none depart,
Awed for myself, and pitying my race,
Our common sorrow, like a mighty wave,
Swept all my pride away, and trembling I forgave!

John Greenleaf Whittier (1807–92)

One Way of Love

All June I bound the rose in sheaves.
Now, rose by rose, I strip the leaves
And strow them where Pauline may pass.
She will not turn aside? Alas!
Let them lie. Suppose they die?
The chance was they might take her eye.

How many a month I strove to suit
These stubborn fingers to the lute!
Today I venture all I know.
She will not hear my music? So!
Break the string; fold music's wing:
Suppose Pauline had bade me sing!

My whole life long I learn'd to love.
This hour my utmost art I prove
And speak my passion–heaven or hell?
She will not give me heaven? 'Tis well!
Lose who may–I still can say,
Those who win heaven, bless'd are they!

Robert Browning (1812–89)

'Justine, You Love Me Not!'

I know, Justine, you speak me fair
As often as we meet;
And 'tis a luxury, I swear,
To hear a voice so sweet;
And yet it does not please me quite,
The civil way you've got;
For me you're something too polite
Justine, you love me not!

I know Justine, you never scold
At aught that I may do:
If I am passionate or cold,
'Tis all the same to you.
'A charming temper,' say the men,
'To smooth a husband's lot':
I wish 'twere ruffled now and then
Justine you love me not!

I know, Justine, you wear a smile
As beaming as the sun;
But who supposes all the while
It shines for only one?
Though azure skies are fair to see,
A transient cloudy spot
In yours would promise more to me
Justine, you love me not!

I know, Justine, you make my name
Your eulogistic theme,
And say - if any chance to blame
You hold me in esteem.
Such words, for all their kindly scope,
Delight me not a jot;
Just as you would have praised the Pope
Justine, you love me not!

I know, Justine - for I have heard
What friendly voices tell
You do not blush to say the word,
'You like me passing well';
And thus the fatal sound I hear
That seals my lonely lot:
There's nothing now to hope or fear
Justine, you love me not!

John Godfrey Saxe (1816–87)

For Each Ecstatic Instant

For each ecstatic instant
We must an anguish pay
In keen and quivering ratio
To the Ecstasy.

For each beloved hour
Sharp pittances of years,
Bitter contested farthings
And coffers heaped with tears.

Emily Dickinson (1830–86)

Love Lies Bleeding

Love lies bleeding in the bed whereover
Roses lean with smiling mouths or pleading:
Earth lies laughing where the sun's dart clove her:
Love lies bleeding.

Stately shine his purple plumes, exceeding
Pride of princes: nor shall maid or lover
Find on earth a fairer sign worth heeding.

Yet may love, sore wounded scarce recover
Strength and spirit again, with life receding:
Hope and joy, wind-winged, about him hover:
Love lies bleeding.

Algernon Charles Swinburne (1837–1909)

Amabel

I marked her ruined hues,
Her custom-straitened views,
And asked, 'Can there indwell
My Amabel?'

I looked upon her gown,
Once rose, now earthen brown;
The change was like the knell
Of Amabel.

Her step's mechanic ways
Had lost the life of May's;
Her laugh, once sweet in swell,
Spoilt Amabel.

I mused: 'Who sings the strain
I sang ere warmth did wane?
Who thinks its numbers spell
His Amabel?'–

Knowing that, though Love cease,
Love's race shows undecrease;
All find in dorp or dell
An Amabel.

I felt that I could creep
To some housetop, and weep,
That Time the tyrant fell
Ruled Amabel!

I said (the while I sighed
That love like ours had died),
'Fond things I'll no more tell
To Amabel,'

'But leave her to her fate,
And fling across the gate,
'Till the Last Trump, farewell,
O Amabel!'

Thomas Hardy (1840–1928)

Hast Thou Forgotten Me?

Hast thou forgotten me? the days are dark
Light ebbs from heaven, and songless soars the lark
Vexed like my heart, loud moans the unquiet sea
Hast thou forgotten me?

Hast thou forgotten me? O dead delight
Whose dreams and memories torture me to-night
O love—my life! O sweet—so fair to see
Hast thou forgotten me?

Hast thou forgotten? Lo, if one should say
Noontide were night, or night were flaming day
Grief blinds mine eyes, I know not which it be!
Hast thou forgotten me?

Hast thou forgotten? Ah, if Death should come,
Close my sad eyes, and charm my song-bird dumb
Tired of strange woes—my fate were hailed with glee
Hast thou forgotten me?

Hast thou forgotten me? What joy have I?
A dim blown bird beneath an alien sky,
O that on mighty pinions I could flee
Hast thou forgotten me?

Hast thou forgotten? Yea, Love's horoscope
Is blurred with tears and suffering beyond Hope
Ah, like dead leaves forsaken of the tree,
Thou hast forgotten me.

Philip Joseph Holdsworth (1849–1902)

Love, What is Love?

Love—what is love? A great and aching heart;
Wrung hands; and silence; and a long despair.
Life—what is life? Upon a moorland bare
To see love coming and see love depart.

Robert Louis Stevenson (1850–94)

The Night Has a Thousand Eyes

The night has a thousand eyes,
And the day but one;
Yet the light of the bright world dies
With the dying sun.

The mind has a thousand eyes,
And the heart but one:
Yet the light of a whole life dies
When love is done.

F.W. Bourdillon (1852–1921)

Desire

Soul of the leaping flame;
Heart of the scarlet fire,
Spirit that hath for name
Only the name, Desire!

Subtle art thou and strong;
Glowing in sunlit skies;
Sparkling in wine and song;
Shining in women's eyes;

Gleaming on shores of Sleep
Moon of the wild dream-clan
Burning within the deep
Passionate heart of Man.

Spirit we can but name,
Essence of Forms that seem,
Odour of violet flame,
Weaver of Thought and Dream.

Laught of the World's great Heart,
Who shall thy rune recote?
Child of the gods thou art,
Offspring of Day and Night.

Lord of the Rainbow realm,
Many a shape hast thou
Glory with laurelled helm;
Love with the myrtled brow;

Sanctity, robed in white;
Liberty, proud and calm,
Ringed wth auroral light,
Bearing the sword and palm.

Maidens with dreamful eyes
Eyes of a dreaming dove,
See thee in noble guise
Coming, and call thee Love!

Youth with his blood aflame,
Running in crystal red,
Sees, on the Mount of Fame,
Thee with thy hands outspread.

Leader of Hope Forlorn,
When he beholds thine eyes
Shining in splendid scorn,
Storming the rampart dies.

Many have, by good hap,
Seen thee in arms arrayed,
Wearing a Phyrian cap,
High on a barricade;

Aye, and by dome and arch
Leading, with eyes ablaze,
Onward the Patriots' March,
Singing the Marseillaise.

Lo, where with trembling lyre
Held in his long white hands
Thrilled by thy glance of fire,
Rapt the Musician stands;

Feeling them all around
Glow in the quiv'ring air
Luminous Soul of Sound!
Music of all things fair!

Poet, and Sage, and Seer,
Smile when the world grows wan,
Knowing thine advent near,
Over the Hills of Dawn.

Anchorite, aple and worn,
Sees thee, and earth disowns
Lifted on prayer, and borne
Up to the Shining Thrones.

Yea, as a seraph-star
Chanting in ecstasy,
Singing in fire afar,
So he beholdeth thee.

And, as in darksome mines,
far down a corridor,
Starlike a small lamp shines,
Raying along the floor

So, ere his race be ran,
Parted his last faint breath,
Thou, for the dying man,
Lightest the ways of Death;

And, while his kindred mourn
Over his shell of clay,
Shinest beyond the bourne,
Dawn of his first new day.

Thus through the lives to be
We shall fare, each alone,
Evermore lured by thee
Unto an End unknown.

Victor James Daley (1858–1905)

Love Walked Alone

Love walked alone.
The rocks cut her tender feet,
And the brambles tore her fair limbs.
There came a companion to her,
But, alas, he was no help,
For his name was heart's pain.

Stephen Crane (1871–1900)

Tell Me Why

Tell me why, behind thee,
I see always the shadow of another lover?
Is it real
Or is this the thrice-damned memory of a better happiness?
Plague on him if he be dead
Plague on him if he be alive
A swinish numbskull
To intrude his shade
Always between me and my peace.

Stephen Crane (1871–1900)

Love One Another

Love one another, but make not a bond of love
Let it rather be a moving sea between the shores of your souls.

Fill each other's cup, but drink not from one cup.
Give one another of your bread, but eat not from the same loaf.

Sing and dance together and be joyous,
but let each one of you be alone,
Even as the strings of a lute are alone
though they quiver with the same music.

Give your hearts, but not into each other's keeping;
For only the hand of Life can contain your hearts.

And stand together yet not too near together;
For the pillars of the temple stand apart,
And the oak tree and the cypress grow not in each other's
shadow.

Khalil Gibran (1883–1931)

LOST LOVE AND
REMEMBRANCE

Eternity of Love Protested

How ill doth he deserve a Lover's name,
Whose pale weak flame
Cannot retain
His heat in spight of absence or disdain;
But doth at once, like paper set on fire,
Burn and expire;
True love can never change his seat,
Nor did he ever love, that could retreat.

That noble flame, which my brest keeps alive,
Shall still survive,
When my soule's fled;
Nor shall my love dye, when my bodye's dead,
That shall wait on me to the lower shade,
And never fade:
My very ashes in their urn,
Shall, like a hallowed Lamp, for ever burn.

Thomas Carew (1595–1640)

To Mary

The twentieth year is well nigh past
Since first our sky was overcast;
Ah would that this might be the last!
My Mary!

Thy spirits have a fainter flow,
I see thee daily weaker grow;
'Twas my distress that brought thee low,
My Mary!

Thy needles, once a shining store,
For my sake restless heretofore,
Now rust disused, and shine no more,
My Mary!

For though thou gladly wouldst fulfil
The same kind office for me still,
Thy sight now seconds not thy will,
My Mary!

But well thou playedst the housewife's part,
And all thy threads with magic art
Have wound themselves about this heart,
My Mary!

Thy indistinct expressions seem
Like language uttered in a dream;
Yet me they charm, whate'er the theme,
My Mary!

Thy silver locks, once auburn bright,
Are still more lovely in my sight
Than golden beams of orient light,
My Mary!

For could I view nor them nor thee,
What sight worth seeing could I see?
The sun would rise in vain for me,
My Mary!

Partakers of thy sad decline,
Thy hands their little force resign;
Yet gently pressed, press gently mine,
My Mary!

Such feebleness of limbs thou prov'st
That now at every step thou mov'st
Upheld by two; yet still thou lov'st,
My Mary!

And still to love, though pressed with ill,
In wintry age to feel no chill,
With me is to be lovely still,
My Mary!

But ah! by constant heed I know
How oft the sadness that I show
Transforms thy smiles to looks of woe,
My Mary!

And should my future lot be cast
With much resemblance of the past,
Thy worn-out heart will break at last,
My Mary!

William Cowper (1731–1800)

Never Seek to Tell Thy Love

Never seek to tell thy love,
Love that never told can be;
For the gentle wind does move
Silently, invisibly.

I told my love, I told my love.
I told her all my heart,
Trembling, cold, in ghastly fears
Ah, she doth depart.

Soon as she was gone from me
A traveler came by
Silently, invisibly
He took her with a sigh. O, was no deny.

William Blake (1757–1827)

I Hid My Love

I hid my love when young till I
Couldn't bear the buzzing of a fly;
I hid my love to my despite
Till I could not bear to look at light:
I dare not gaze upon her face
But left her memory in each place;
Where'er I saw a wild flower lie
I kissed and bade my love good-bye.

I met her in the greenest dells,
Where dewdrops pearl the wood bluebells;
The lost breeze kissed her bright blue eye,
The bee kissed and went singing by,
A sunbeam found a passage there,
A gold chain round her neck so fair;
As secret as the wild bee's song
She lay there all the summer long.

I hid my love in field and town
Till e'en the breeze would knock me down;
The bees seemed singing ballads o'er,
The fly's bass turned a lion's roar;
And even silence found a tongue,
To haunt me all the summer long;
The riddle nature could not prove
Was nothing else but secret love.

John Clare (1793–1864)

Why is the Rose so Pale?

Oh Dearest, canst thou tell me why
The Rose should be so pale?
And why the azure Violet
Should wither in the vale?

And why the Lark should, in the cloud,
So sorrowfully sing?
And why from loveliest balsam-buds
A scent of death should spring?

And why the Sun upon the mead
So chillingly should frown?
And why the Earth should, like a grave,
Be mouldering and brown?

And why is it that I, myself,
So languishing should be?
And why is it, my Heart-of-Hearts,
That thou forsakest me?

Heinrich Heine (1797–1856)

I Loved You Once

I loved you once, nor can this heart be quiet;
For it would seem that love still lingers there;
But do not you be further troubled by it;
I would in no wise hurt you, oh, my dear.

I loved you without hope, a mute offender;
What jealous pangs, what shy despairs I knew!
A love as deep as this, as true, as tender,
God grant another may yet offer you.

Alexander Sergeyvich Pushkin (1799–1837)

If We Should Ever Meet Again

If we should ever meet again
When many tedious years are past;
When time shall have unbound the chain,
And this sad heart is free at last;
Then shall we meet and look unmov'd,
As though we ne'er had met—had lov'd!
And I shall mark without a tear
How cold and calm thy alter'd brow;
I shall forget thou once wert dear,
Rememb'ring but thy broken vow!
Rememb'ring that in trusting youth
I lov'd thee with the purest truth;
That now the fleeting dream is o'er,
And thou canst raise the spell no more!

Louisa Stuart Costello (1799–1870)

Tomorrow at Dawn

Tomorrow, at dawn, at the hour when the countryside whitens,
I will set out. You see, I know that you wait for me.
I will go by the forest, I will go by the mountain.
I can no longer remain far from you.

I will walk with my eyes fixed on my thoughts,
Seeing nothing of outdoors, hearing no noise
Alone, unknown, my back curved, my hands crossed,
Sorrowed, and the day for me will be as the night.

I will not look at the gold of evening which falls,
Nor the distant sails going down towards Harfleur,
And when I arrive, I will place on your tomb
A bouquet of green holly and of flowering heather.

Victor Hugo (1802–85)

At Last

O the years I lost before I knew you, Love!
O, the hills I climbed and came not to you, Love!
Ah! who shall render unto us to make us glad
The things which for and of each other's sake
We might have had?

If you and I had sat and played together, Love,
Two speechless babes in the summer weather, Love,
By one sweet brook which, though it dried up long ago,
Still makes for me today a sweeter song
Than all I know—

If hand-in-hand through the mysterious gateway, Love
Of womanhood, we had first looked and straightway, Love,
Had whispered to each other softly, ere it yet
Was dawn, what now in noonday heat and fear
We both forget—

If all of this had given its completeness, Love,
To every hour, would it be added sweetness, Love?
Or ill with thee? One wish could I more sweetly tell,
More swift fulfill?

Ah, vainly thus I sit and dream and ponder, Love,
Losing the precious present while I wonder, Love,
About the days in which you grew and came
To be so beautiful, and did not know the name
Or sight of me.

But all lost things are in the angel's keeping, Love;
No past is dead for us, but only sleeping, Love;
The years of heaven will all earth's little pain make good,
Together there we can begin again, in babyhood.

Helen Hunt Jackson (1830–85)

The First Day

I wish I could remember the first day,
First hour, first moment of your meeting me,
If bright or dim the season, it might be
Summer or Winter for aught I can say.
So unrecorded did it slip away,
So blind was I to see and forsee,
So dull to mark the budding of my tree
That would not blossom yet for many a May.
If only I could recollect it, such
A day of days! I let it come and go
As traceless as a thaw of bygone snow;
It seemed to mean so little, meant so much;
If only now I could recall that touch,
First touch of hand in hand – Did one but know!

Christina Georgina Rossetti (1830–94)

Remember

Remember me when I am gone away,
   Gone far away into the silent land;
   When you can no more hold me by the hand,
Nor I half turn to go yet turning to stay.
Remember me when no more day by day
   You tell me of our future that you plann'd:
   Only remember me; you understand
It will be late to counsel then or pray.

Yet if you should forget me for a while
   And afterwards remember, do not grieve:
   For if the darkness and corruption leave
   A vestige of the thoughts that once I had,
Better by far you should forget and smile
   Than that you should remember and be sad.

Christina Georgina Rossetti (1830–94)

Our Hands Have Met

Our hands have met, our lips have met
Our souls—who knows when the wind blows
How light souls drift mid longings set,
If thou forget'st, can I forget
The time that was not long ago?

Thou wert not silent then, but told
Sweet secrets dear—I drew so near
Thy shamefaced cheeks grown overbold,
That scarce thine eyes might I behold!
Ah was it then so long ago!

Trembled my lips and thou wouldst turn
But hadst no heart to draw apart,
Beneath my lips thy cheek did burn—
Yet no rebuke that I might learn;
Yea kind looks still, not long ago.

Wilt thou be glad upon the day
When unto me this love shall be
An idle fancy passed away,
And we shall meet and smile and say
'O wasted sighs of long ago!'

Wilt thou rejoice that thou hast set
Cold words, dull shows 'twixt hearts drawn close,
That cold at heart I live on yet,
Forgetting still that I forget
The priceless days of long ago?

William Morris (1834–96)

Farewell

Farewell: we two shall still meet day by day,
Live side by side;
But never more shall heart respond to heart.
Two stranger boats can drift adown one tide,
Two branches on one stem grow green apart.
Farewell, I say.

Farewell: chance travellers, as the path they tread,
Change words and smile,
And share their travellers' fortunes, friend with friend,
And yet are foreign in their thoughts the while,
Several, alone, save that one way they wend.
Farewell; 'tis said.

Farewell: ever the bitter asphodel
Outlives love's rose;
The fruit and blossom of the dead for us.
Ah, answer me, should this have been the close,
To be together and be sundered thus?
But yet, farewell.

Augusta Davies Webster (1837–94)

A Broken Appointment

You did not come,
And marching Time drew on, and wore me numb.
Yet less for loss of your dear presence there
Than that I thus found lacking in your make
That high compassion which can overbear
Reluctance for pure lovingkindness' sake
Grieved I, when, as the hope-hour stroked its sum,
You did not come.

You love me not,
And love alone can lend you loyalty;
I know and knew it. But, unto the store
Of human deeds divine in all but name,
Was it not worth a little hour or more
To add yet this: Once you, a woman, came
To soothe a time-torn man; even though it be
You love me not.

Thomas Hardy (1840–1928)

A Wife in London

She sits in the tawny vapour
That the Thames-side lanes have uprolled,
Behind whose webby fold-on-fold
Like a waning taper
The street-lamp glimmers cold.

A messenger's knock cracks smartly,
Flashed news in her hand
Of meaning it dazes to understand
Though shaped so shortly:
He–he has fallen–in the far South Land...

'Tis the morrow; the fog hangs thicker,
The postman nears and goes:
A letter is brought whose lines disclose
By the firelight flicker
His hand, whom the worm now knows:

Fresh–firm–penned in highest feather–
Page-full of his hoped return,
And of home-planned jaunts of brake and burn
In the summer weather,
And of new love that they would learn.

Thomas Hardy (1840–1928)

The Voice

Woman much missed, how you call to me, call to me,
Saying that now you are not as you were
When you had changed from the one who was all to me,
But as at first, when our day was fair.

Can it be you that I hear? Let me view you, then.
Standing as when I drew near to the town
Where you would wait for me: yes, as I knew you then,
Even to the original air-blue gown!

Or is it only the breeze, in its listlessness
Travelling across the wet mead to me here,
You being ever dissolved to wan wistlessness,
Heard no more again far or near?

  Thus I; faltering forward,
  Leaves around me falling,
Wind oozing thin through the thorn from norward,
  And the woman calling.

Thomas Hardy (1840–1928)

The Time of the Rose is Over

Love, turn thy gentle feet away,
How can I be thy lover?
The years pass onward to decay
And the bloom of the rose is over.

The sweet light fails from out the sky,
The weary wind is wailing,
The rain, like tears, is falling nigh
From the grey cloud o'er us sailing.

O rare, glad time when youth was sweet
With all its pulses beating,
When music led thy gentle feet,
And a rainbow was o'er our meeting.

The rose was bright, but brighter still,
The eyes that shone like heaven;
O Love, come back again and thrill
Our souls like a soul forgiven.

When heart to heart spoke soft and low,
As lovers' words are spoken.
When truth was truth and youth was youth,
And never a vow was broken.

Love, turn thy gentle feet away,
How can I be thy lover?
A low wind grieves among the leaves,
And the time of the rose is over.

Alexander Anderson (1845–1909)

Renouncement

I must not think of thee; and, tired yet strong,
I shun the love that lurks in all delight–
The love of thee–and in the blue heaven's height,
And in the dearest passage of a song.
Oh, just beyond the sweetest thoughts that throng
This breast, the thought of thee waits hidden yet bright;
But it must never, never come in sight;
I must stop short of thee the whole day long.
But when sleep comes to close each difficult day,
When night gives pause to the long watch I keep,
And all my bonds I needs must loose apart,
Must doff my will as raiment laid away,–
With the first dream that comes with the first sleep
I run, I run, I am gather'd to thy heart.

Alice Meynell (1847–1922)

A Love by the Sea

Out of the starless night that covers me,
(O tribulation of the wind that rolls!)
Black as the cloud of some tremendous spell,
The susurration of the sighing sea
Sounds like the sobbing whisper of two souls
That tremble in a passion of farewell.

To the desires that trebled life in me,
(O melancholy of the wind that rolls!)
The dreams that seemed the future to foretell,
The hopes that mounted herward like the sea,
To all the sweet things sent on happy souls,
I cannot choose but bid a mute farewell.

And to the girl who was so much to me
(O lamentation of this wind that rolls!)
Since I may not the life of her compel,
Out of the night, beside the sounding sea,
Full of the love that might have blent our souls,
A sad, a last, a long, supreme farewell.

William Ernest Henley (1849–1903)

Missing

You walked beside me, quick and free;
With lingering touch you grasped my hand;
Your eyes looked laughingly in mine;
And now—I can not understand.

I long for you, I mourn for you,
Through all the dark and lonely hours.
Heavy the weight the pallmen lift,
And cover silently with flowers.

Sarah Orne Jewett (1849–1909)

Do You think that I do not know?

They say that I never have written of love,
As a writer of songs should do;
They say that I never could touch the strings
With a touch that is firm and true;
They say I know nothing of women and men
In the fields where Love's roses grow,
And they say I must write with a halting pen
Do you think that I do not know?

When the love-burst came, like an English Spring,
In days when our hair was brown,
And the hem of her skirt was a sacred thing
And her hair was an angel's crown.
The shock when another man touched her arm,
Where the dancers sat round in a row;
The hope and despair, and the false alarm
Do you think that I do not know?

By the arbour lights on the western farms,
You remember the question put,
While you held her warm in your quivering arms
And you trembled from head to foot.
The electric shock from her finger tips,
And the murmuring answer low,
The soft, shy yielding of warm red lips
Do you think that I do not know?

She was buried at Brighton, where Gordon sleeps,
When I was a world away;
And the sad old garden its secret keeps,
For nobody knows to-day.

She left a message for me to read,
Where the wild wide oceans flow;
Do you know how the heart of a man can bleed
Do you think that I do not know?

I stood by the grave where the dead girl lies,
When the sunlit scenes were fair,
And the white clouds high in the autumn skies,
And I answered the message there.
But the haunting words of the dead to me
Shall go wherever I go.
She lives in the Marriage that Might Have Been
Do you think that I do not know?

They sneer or scoff, and they pray or groan,
And the false friend plays his part.
Do you think that the blackguard who drinks alone
Knows aught of a pure girl's heart?
Knows aught of the first pure love of a boy
With his warm young blood aglow,
Knows aught of the thrill of the world-old joy
Do you think that I do not know?

They say that I never have written of love,
They say that my heart is such
That finer feelings are far above;
But a writer may know too much.
There are darkest depths in the brightest nights,
When the clustering stars hang low;
There are things it would break his strong heart to write
Do you think that I do not know?

Henry Lawson (1867–1922)

No One so Much as You

No one so much as you
Loves this my clay,
Or would lament as you
Its dying day.

You know me through and through
Though I have not told,
And though with what you know
You are not bold.

None ever was so fair
As I thought you:
Not a word can I bear
Spoken against you.

All that I ever did
For you seemed coarse
Compared with what I hid
Nor put in force.

My eyes scarce dare meet you
Lest they should prove
I but respond to you
And do not love.

We look and understand,
We cannot speak
Except in trifles and
Words the most weak.

For I at most accept
Your love, regretting
That is all: I have kept
Only a fretting

That I could not return
All that you gave
And could not ever burn
With the love you have,

Till sometimes it did seem
Better it were
Never to see you more
Than linger here

With only gratitude
Instead of love
A pine in solitude
Cradling a dove.

Edward Thomas (1878–1917)

Extract from The Great Lover

I have been so great a lover: filled my days
So proudly with the splendour of Love's praise,
The pain, the calm, and the astonishment,
Desire illimitable, and still content,
And all dear names men use, to cheat despair,
For the perplexed and viewless streams that bear
Our hearts at random down the dark of life.
Now, ere the unthinking silence on that strife
Steals down, I would cheat drowsy Death so far,
My night shall be remembered for a star
That outshone all the suns of all men's days.
Shall I not crown them with immortal praise
Whom I have loved, who have given me, dared with me
High secrets, and in darkness knelt to see
The inenarrable godhead of delight?
Love is a flame; we have beaconed the world's night.

Rupert Brooke (1887–1915)

The Meeting

We started speaking,
Looked at each other, then turned away.
The tears kept rising to my eyes.
But I could not weep.
I wanted to take your hand
But my hand trembled.
You kept counting the days
Before we should meet again.
But both of us felt in our hearts
That we parted for ever and ever.
The ticking of the little clock filled the quiet room.
'Listen,' I said. 'It is so loud,
Like a horse galloping on a lonely road,
As loud as a horse galloping past in the night.'
You shut me up in your arms.
But the sound of the clock stifled our hearts' beating.
You said, 'I cannot go: all that is living of me
Is here for ever and ever.'
Then you went.
The world changed. The sound of the clock grew fainter,
Dwindled away, became a minute thing.
I whispered in the darkness. 'If it stops, I shall die.'

Katherine Mansfield (1888–1923)

My Grandmother's Love Letters

There are no stars to-night
But those of memory.
Yet how much room for memory there is
In the loose girdle of soft rain.

There is even room enough
For the letters of my mother's mother, Elizabeth,
That have been pressed so long
Into a corner of the roof
That they are brown and soft,
And liable to melt as snow.

Over the greatness of such space
Steps must be gentle.
It is all hung by an invisible white hair.
It trembles as birch limbs webbing the air.

And I ask myself:
'Are your fingers long enough to play
Old keys that are but echoes:
Is the silence strong enough
To carry back the music to its source
And back to you again
As though to her?'

Yet I would lead my grandmother by the hand
Through much of what she would not understand;
And so I stumble. And the rain continues on the roof
With such a sound of gently pitying laughter.

Harold Hart Crane (1899–1932)

Picture Credits

10–11 after William Adolphe Bouguereau (1825–1905) Cupid and Psyche, c. 1889 © Sotheby's Picture Library

12–13 William Holman Hunt (1827–1910) Our English Coasts, 1852 Courtesy of the Tate Gallery

14 Sir John Everett Millais (1829–96) Autumn Leaves, 1855–56 Courtesy of Topham Picturepoint

16 Sir Edward Coley Burne-Jones (1833–98) Pygmalion and Galatea II: The Hand Refrains, 1875–78 Courtesy of Birmingham Museums and Art Gallery

18 Fritz Zuber-Bühler (1822–96) The Spirit of the Morning © Sotheby's Picture Library

21 Edward Robert Hughes (1849–1914) Night © Sotheby's Picture Library

23 Sir Joseph Noël Paton (1821–1901) How an Angel Rowed Sir Galahad Across Dern Mere © The Fine Art Society, London, UK/The Bridgeman Art Library

25 William Holman Hunt (1827–1910) The Hireling Shepherd, 1851 Courtesy of Topham Picturepoint

26 Edward John Poynter (1836–1919) At Low Tide, c. 1913 Courtesy of Christie's Images Ltd

29 Dante Gabriel Rossetti (1828–82) La Ghirlandata, 1873 Courtesy of Giraudon/The Bridgeman Art Library

30–31 Dante Gabriel Rossetti (1828–82) Paolo and Francesca da Rimini, 1855 Courtesy of the Tate Gallery

32 Léon Jean Basile Perrault (1832–1908) Cupid's Arrow, 1882 © Sotheby's Picture Library

35 Léon Jean Basile Perrault (1832–1908) The Sleeping Angel, 1897 © Sotheby's Picture Library

36 Richard Dadd (1817–86) Titania Sleeping, c. 1841 © Christie's Images Ltd

38–39 Alexandre Cabanel (1823–89) The Birth of Venus, 1863 © Sotheby's Picture Library

40–41 John Roddam Spencer Stanhope (1829–1908) Love and the Maiden, 1877 Courtesy of Christie's Images Ltd

42–43 François Boucher (1703–70) La Cible d'Amour (The Target of Love), 1758 Courtesy of Private Collection/Christie's Images Ltd

45 Dante Gabriel Rossetti (1828–82) Lucrezia Borgia, c. 1861 Courtesy of the Tate Gallery

46 Gustav Klimt (1862–1918) The Kiss, 1907–08 Courtesy of Osterreichische Galerie, Vienna, Austria/The Bridgeman Art Library

48 Dante Gabriel Rossetti (1828–82) Proserpine, 1877 Courtesy of the Tate Gallery

50–51 Eleanor Fortescue Brickdale (1871–1945) The Uninvited Guest, 1906 © Eleanor Fortescue Brickdale/Sotheby's Picture Library

53 Simeon Solomon (1840–1905) Bacchus, 1867 Courtesy of Birmingham Museums and Art Gallery

54 Charles Edward Halle (1846–1919) Paolo and Francesca, 1888 Courtesy of Christie's Images Ltd

57 William Adolphe Bouguereau (1825–1905) L'Innocence, 1890 © Christie's Images Ltd

58 Guillaume Seignac (1870–1924) L'Amour Désarmé © Christie's Images Ltd

61 Guillaume Seignac (1870–1924) The Awakening of Psyche, c. 1904 © Christie's Images Ltd

63 Eleanor Fortescue Brickdale (1871–1945) Natural Magic, c. 1905 Courtesy of Christie's Images Ltd

64 Francisco Goya (1746–1828) The Clothed Maja, c. 1800–05 Courtesy of Prado, Madrid, Spain/The Bridgeman Art Library/Christie's Images Ltd

67 Gustave Doré (1832–83) A Midsummer Night's Dream, c. 1870 © Sotheby's Picture Library

68 Jacques-Clément Wagrez (1846–1908) Eros, 1876 © Sotheby's Picture Library

70–71 Ludwig Knaus (1829–1910) Peace © Sotheby's Picture Library

73 John Atkinson Grimshaw (1836–93) Iris, 1876 © Sotheby's Picture Library

74 Edward Robert Hughes (1849–1914) Midsummer Eve, 1908 © Sotheby's Picture Library

77 Jan Vermeer (1632–75) Girl with a Pearl Earring Courtesy of Mouritshuis, The Hague, Netherlands/The Bridgeman Art Library

78–79 Tintoretto (1518–94) The Concert of Muses Courtesy of Private Collection/Christie's Images

81 Ford Madox Brown (1821–93) Romeo and Juliet, c. 1867 Courtesy of Christie's Images Ltd

82–83 Edgar Degas (1834–1917) Danseuses Vertes, 1878 Courtesy of Private Collection/Christie's Images Ltd

84 Bartolomé Estebán Murillo (1618–82) Immaculate Conception, 1661 Courtesy of Private Collection/Christie's Images Ltd

86 Frederic, Lord Leighton (1830–96) Flaming June, 1895 Courtesy of Christie's Images Ltd

88 Dante Gabriel Rossetti (1828–82) Elizabeth Siddal, c. 1854–55 Courtesy of Christie's Images Ltd

91 Dante Gabriel Rossetti (1828–82) The Beloved, 1865–66 Courtesy of the Tate Gallery

93 Arthur Hughes (1832–1915) April Love, 1855 Courtesy of the Tate Gallery

95 Frederic, Lord Leighton (1830–96) The Painter's Honeymoon, c. 1864 Courtesy of Christie's Images Ltd

99 Simeon Solomon (1840–1905) Dawn, 1871 Courtesy of Birmingham Museums and Art Gallery

100 E. Corbett (née Ellenborough) (dates unknown) The Sleeping Girl Courtesy of Christie's Images Ltd

102–03 Emile Munier (1840–95) La Sauvetage ('The Rescue'), 1894 © NYC Christie's Images Ltd

105 Tintoretto (1518–94) The Concert of Muses Courtesy of Private Collection/Christie's Images

109 Sophie Anderson (1823–1903) Thus Your Fairy's Made of Most Beautiful Things © The Maas Gallery, London, UK/The Bridgeman Art Library

110 John Atkinson Grimshaw (1836–93) Autumn – Dame Autumn Hath a Mournful Face, 1871 © Christie's Images Ltd

113 Angelica Kauffmann (1741–1807) Portrait of a Lady as the Muse Euterpe Courtesy of Private Collection/Christie's Images Ltd

116 Sir John Everett Millais (1829–96) Youth, c. 1847 © Christie's Images Ltd

119 Sir Thomas Lawrence (1769–1830) Portrait of Mrs Robert Burne-Jones Courtesy of Private Collection/Christie's Images Ltd

121 Eleanor Fortescue Brickdale (1871–1945) The Uninvited Guest, 1906 © Eleanor Fortescue Brickdale/Sotheby's Picture Library

127 William Holman Hunt (1827–1910) The Awakening Conscience, 1854 Courtesy of the Tate Gallery

128 Jean-Honoré Fragonard (1732–1806) Les Hazards Heureux de l'Escarpolette ('The Swing'), 1767 Courtesy of Wallace Collection, London, UK/The Bridgeman Art Library

131 Richard Dadd (1817–86) Come unto these yellow sands, 1842 © Private Collection/The Bridgeman Art Library

133 Frederick Sandys (1829–1904) Love's Shadow, 1867 Courtesy of Christie's Images Ltd

136 George Romney (1734–1802) Portrait of Emma, Lady Hamilton, 1786 Courtesy of Philip Mould, Historical Portraits Ltd, London, UK/The Bridgeman Art Library

138 Emile Munier (1840–95) La Sauvetage ('The Rescue'), 1894 © NYC Christie's Images Ltd

141 Dante Gabriel Rossetti (1828–82) Reverie, 1868 Courtesy of Christie's Images Ltd

146 after William Adolphe Bouguereau (1825–1905) Cupid and Psyche, c. 1889 © Sotheby's Picture Library

149 John William Waterhouse (1849–1917) Ophelia, c. 1894 Courtesy of Private Collection/Christie's Images Ltd

150 Dante Gabriel Rossetti (1828–82) Study for Delia, c. 1853–55 Courtesy of Birmingham Museums and Art Gallery

153 Dante Gabriel Rossetti (1828–82) Venus Verticordia, 1867 Courtesy of Christie's Images Ltd

154–55 Sandro Botticelli (1445–1510) The Birth of Venus, c. 1485 Courtesy of Galleria Degli Uffizi, Florence/The Bridgeman Art Library/Christie's Images Ltd

159 Dante Gabriel Rossetti (1828–82) Beata Beatrix, 1870 Courtesy of the Tate Gallery

160 Solomon Joseph Solomon (1860–1927) Laus Deo! © Sotheby's Picture Library

166 Arthur Hughes (1832–1915) The Long Engagement, 1853–59 Courtesy of Birmingham Museums and Art Gallery

171 Ludwig Knaus (1829–1910) Peace © Sotheby's Picture Library

172 John Roddam Spencer Stanhope (1829–1908) Thoughts of the Past, 1859 Courtesy of the Tate Gallery

174–75 A.C. Lalli, after Dante Gabriel Rossetti (1828–82) Dante's Dream at the Time of the Death of Beatrice, c. 1900 © Christie's Images Ltd

176 Anna Lea Merritt (1844–1930) Love Locked Out, 1889 Courtesy of the Tate Gallery

181 Sir Edward Coley Burne-Jones (1833–98) Hill Fairies, c. 1881 © Christie's Images Ltd

183 Charles Sims (1873–1928) Titania's Awakening, 1896 © Christie's Images Ltd

184 William Holman Hunt (1827–1910) Isabella and the Pot of Basil, 1866–68 Courtesy of Tyne and Wear Museums Service

188–89 Sir Joseph Noël Paton (1821–1901) Cymolchles and Phaedria Crossing the Lake of Idleness in an Enchanted Boat © Sotheby's Picture Library

191 John William Waterhouse (1849–1917) Miranda: The Tempest, 1916 Courtesy of Christie's Images Ltd

194 Dante Gabriel Rossetti (1828–82) La Ghirlandata, 1873 Courtesy of Giraudon/The Bridgeman Art Library

197 Eugène Medard (1847–87) L'Amour et Psyche ('Cupid and Psyche') © Sotheby's Picture Library

198 Frederic, Lord Leighton (1830–96) Flaming June, 1895 Courtesy of Christie's Images Ltd

201 Sir Edward Coley Burne-Jones (1833–98) Pygmalion and Galatea IV: The Soul Attains, 1875–78 Courtesy of Birmingham Museums and Art Gallery

202 Sandro Botticelli (1445–1510) The Birth of Venus, c. 1485 Courtesy of Galleria Degli Uffizi, Florence/The Bridgeman Art Library/Christie's Images Ltd

205 Charles Edward Hallé (1846–1919) Luna, c. 1870s–80s Courtesy of Christie's Images Ltd

Tintoretto (1518–94) The Concert of Muses Courtesy of Private Collection/Christie's Images

207 Frederic, Lord Leighton (1830–96) The Painter's Honeymoon, c. 1864 Courtesy of Christie's Images Ltd

208–09 Richard Dadd (1817–86) Come unto these yellow sands, 1842 © Private Collection/The Bridgeman Art Library

Index of Titles

Index of Poets